Behind Castle Walls

at Sudeley Past and Present

ELIZABETH ASHCOMBE

Elizabeth Ashcombe

AMBERLEY

A History of Sudeley

King Edward VI, granted Sudeley to his uncle, Sir Thomas Seymour.

Seymour married Katherine Parr.

King Ethelred (The Unready) gave the Saxon manor house and estate at Sudeleagh to his daughter Goda, sister of King Edward the Confessor, on her marriage to Walter de Maunt.

1000

Harold was succeeded by his son John de Sudeley.

1085

Ralph de Sudeley succeeded to Sudeley Castle and gave Toddington to his brother William, who assumed his mother's name of Tracy and was the ancestor of the present Tracy family.

1165

John 9th Lord de Sudeley was killed in Spain while fighting for the Black Prince. His nephew Ralph Boteler inherited Sudeley.

1367

Wars of the Roses. Edward IV of the House of York came to power and Boteler was forced to sell Sudeley Castle to the King.

Richard acceded to the throne as Richard III and became the owner of Sudeley for the second time.

1469

Katherine gave birth to a daughter, Mary, but died 7 days later of puerperal fever. She was buried in the Chapel of St Mary.

1547

1066

Norman Conquest, Ralf's son Harold was allowed to retain Sudeley but deprived of his earldom by William the Conqueror.

1139

During the reign of King Stephen the Sudeley manor house was fortified. John revolted against the King. Stephen seized Sudeley and made it a royal garrison – first destruction of the Castle.

1170

William de Tracy was one of the four knights who murdered Thomas à Becket in Canterbury Cathedral.

1442

Boteler built Sudeley Castle on its present site using his spoils from the Hundred Years War with France. The Chapel (now St Mary's Church) and the Tithe Barn were also built at this time.

1483

Richard III defeated and killed in the Battle of Bosworth bringing to an end the Wars of the Roses and the House of York.

Henry VII, the new monarch granted Sudeley to his uncle and staunch supporter, Jasper Tudor, Duke of Bedford

1549

Seymour was executed after being indicted on 33 counts of 'Treason and other Misdemeanours' against King and Crown.

Mary I granted the Castle and manor of Sudeley to Baron Chandos of Sudeley. His descendants held Sudeley for the next 100 years.

In 1572 Edmund 2nd Lord Chandos carried out extensive alterations and additions to the Castle.

1554

For two centuries the ruins of Sudeley lay neglected and left to the ravages of the weather, its stones plundered by local builders. The title and estates changed hands many times and what little remained of the Castle was occupied by the tenants of the surrounding estate and was also at one time an inn, The Castle Arms.

1655

John and William Dent bought the Castle from the Duke of Buckingham and Chandos.

With architect Harvey Eginton, the Dents completed the restoration of the Elizabethan ranges of the outer courtyard.

1837

Emma Dent died and the Castle was inherited by her nephew Henry Dent Brocklehurst. The Dent-Brocklehursts have held Sudeley in unbroken succession since that time.

Major Dent-Brocklehurst took over Sudeley.

1927

Mark and his wife Elizabeth succeeded his mother as owners of Sudeley and decided the only hope for its survival was to open the Castle to the public. It took two years and a huge upheaval to adapt Sudeley from merely a family home to a tourist attraction.

1969

Elizabeth Dent-Brocklehurst married Lord Ashcombe and in the early 1980s they carried out a further major refurbishment in an attempt to strike a balance between a visitor attraction and what remains primarily a family home. Her children, Henry and Mollie Dent-Brocklehurst have now taken over the management of the visitor attraction.

1979

1643

Sudeley was surrendered after a three day siege to Colonel Massey and his Roundhead troops.

In April Sudeley was re-garrisoned by Lord Chandos and in September, after the Royalist defeat at Gloucester, King Charles made it his headquarters.

1810

Lord Rivers of Stratfield Saye sold the Castle to the Marquis of Buckingham, afterwards Duke of Buckingham and Chandos.

1855

Sudeley inherited by the Dent's nephew John Coucher Dent who had married Emma Brocklehurst daughter of John Brocklehurst.

The Victorian architect George Gilbert Scott employed to restore the Sudeley Chapel.

1941

A Prisoner of War camp for Italians and Germans sited in the Castle grounds.

Mark Dent-Brocklehurst inherited Sudeley on the death of his father, but his mother Mary Dent-Brocklehurst continued to live in the Castle until 1969.

1972

Mark Dent-Brocklehurst died and once again Sudeley was beset by more death duties and massive debts. His widow took on sole responsibility for the Castle and began a 20th century renaissance of the property.

Mark, Lucien, Luca, Violet and Jake,
my grandchildren

Front cover illustration: copyright © Les Wilson.

This edition first published 2009

Amberley Publishing Plc
Cirencester Road, Chalford,
Stroud, Gloucestershire, GL6 8PE

www.amberleybooks.com

Copyright © Elizabeth Ashcombe, 2009

The right of Elizabeth Ashcombe to be identified as the Author
of this work has been asserted in accordance with the
Copyrights, Designs and Patents Act 1988.

British Library Cataloguing in Publication Data.
A catalogue record for this book is available from the British Library.

ISBN 978 1 84868 801 8

Typesetting and Origination by Diagraf (www.diagraf.net)
Printed in Great Britain

Contents

Acknowledgements

This has been in many ways a group project. Jean Bray has researched and assembled all of the historical and archival material; Genie Henderson has generously lent her time and editing skills. Both have tactfully suggested improvements and corrected my spelling and punctuation gaffes. Sarah Lear has tirelessly compiled and copied photographs and drafts and put them into sensible shape. A special thank you to the above mentioned and to all the colourful characters both from the human and animal kingdoms who have played their part in this tale.

Introduction

Several years ago I started to make a record of my life and times at Sudeley with an attempt to bring its history, which spans over 1,000 years, up to date. The last recorded chapter of this epic story ended with the death of Emma Dent in 1900. Emma was Sudeley's nineteenth-century chatelaine and heroine who devoted her enormous energy to the castle, researching and archiving its history and embellishing it with a diverse collection of artefacts, paintings, furniture and textiles ranging from ancient through Tudor, Stuart and Georgian to Victorian times. She also left for posterity a fascinating and illuminating chronicle of her own daily life.

Emma and her husband had no children and after her death the castle and estate passed to her family where it remained through two further generations until inherited by my late husband Mark-Dent Brocklehurst and subsequently by my two children and me in 1972. I had arrived at Sudeley as a bride ten years previously and have now lived within its domain for the best part of half a century, giving me over one hundred years of history, from the beginning of the twentieth century until now, to catch up on. I have been much encouraged and helped in this project by Jean Bray, Sudeley's archivist and published author and biographer of Emma Dent, and my sister Genie Henderson, also a published author. However, despite their proddings, suggestions, deadlines and sighs, not much seemed to be coming off the page. As a newcomer to writing, I was somewhat intimidated by the scope, style and structure of producing a readable book and hadn't realised what a task I had let myself in for.

In the midst of my procrastinations however I was invited to contribute a monthly column to *Cotswold Life* magazine, entitled 'Castle Connections'. It was to be a chatty day-to-day account of the comings and goings at Sudeley with a reflection on the history and the activities and entertainments we offered to our visitors and importantly, each article was to be kept to around 650 words. Well, here was the structure I had been looking for and I soon found that I was enjoying thinking up my monthly theme and writing it. I began hearing from and meeting people who said they were fans of my column, which added encouragement. When it was suggested by Amberley Publishing that we publish a book of the past two years of articles and illustrate them from our own family archives, I accepted enthusiastically, thinking that this should let me off the hook on the bigger assignment. However, apparently it doesn't. It has been suggested that this is to be just a 'taster'.

Sudeley has had an extraordinary history with many of England's most celebrated characters walking on and off the stage through the years: Richard III, Henry VIII, Queen Katherine Parr, Lady Jane Grey and Elizabeth I (to name but a few) have all played their part in our story. It has seen magnificent times and turbulent times but always managed to survive. Jean Bray is constantly finding more intrigues and stories to add to the collection. The twentieth century may not be quite so regal, but it too has seen its good and bad times accompanied by many interesting participants. Today the castle is an active tourist attraction with all its 'finery' on display. It is also our family home, now divided into three independent apartments, where I live in neighbourly proximity to my son and daughter and their families. My five grandchildren are my great joy and I often can't resist mentioning them in my articles. Living amongst all this history and daily activity makes life interesting and at times challenging but like so many of Sudeley's former owners I am fascinated by the castle's past and devoted to its future.

Author's Note

Much of this book was previously published (2007-2009) in *Cotswold Life* as a series of monthly articles entitled 'Castle Connections'. The articles have been edited and in some cases, altered and expanded for this book, and I have also included some original pieces which are not part of the *Cotswold Life* collection.

The Central Courtyard.

Sudeley is an example of how to keep old houses open without loss of dignity. It is conserved largely as it was in Emma Dent's day. To walk the sequence of marquees and stalls, parterres and terraces is to have the illusion of joining in a large house party. The old Tithe Barn has been left an ivy-clad ruin. The double yew hedge of the Queen's Garden is a sumptuous 'room outdoors', its beds of herbs and roses like a giant Persian carpet. Trees are as much part of Sudeley as its architecture.

Extract from England's Best Houses *by Simon Jenkins.*

Autumn

Morning Walk

This the start of my column for *Cotswold Life* magazine in which I hope to bring you a glimpse of life at one of England's oldest and most beautiful castles. I have now lived at Sudeley Castle for over forty years and was married here in the little fifteenth-century church in the garden forty-five years ago. This fact makes me seem rather old; it's challenging with my middle-aged children and five grandchildren to successfully brush that thought under the carpet. And yet the special and ethereal beauty of Sudeley exerts its own timeless magic on all who live here.

I have started to wake up at dawn since my jet-lagged grandchildren arrived from Hawaii, and have taken up early morning bike riding on fine days with six-year-old Mark. Last week we pedalled and pushed around the castle at around 6.30 am and I was completely awestruck by the total magic and beauty of the gardens and surrounding hills, so fresh and alive at that hour: the birdsong, trees, colours, dewdrops on petals, scents, unfolding fields and wakening sheep, all the shades of green and shapes of hedges, accompanied by the lively and enchanting conversation of my grandson.

At first he boasted that his bike was faster than mine, which wasn't true, but I let that one pass. He then informed me that kings and queens used to live at Sudeley, which is true, but they didn't ride bicycles, they had horses and golden carriages with special people to help you up and down. The conversation then turned to the menace or merit of grey squirrels and rabbits, before wandering off into musings of a more metaphysical nature, such as 'where does God live?' When I struggled with the 'he lives here in everything around us' type of reply, Mark interrupted with, 'My Dad (an oft quoted authority on almost everything) said he lives in Devon'. I decided to let that one pass unchallenged as well as it was almost breakfast time but I stand by my version of things as it is moments such as these that keep my spirits fresh and alive.

As a typical day at Sudeley unfolds most of my time is spent behind walls carrying out the many tasks involved in running a large house that is also open to the public. Our aim is to provide a wonderful ambience and experience for our visitors who come to us from all over England and indeed the world. Good intentions aside this isn't always the case and I am collecting reminiscences of some memorable gaffes which have happened during my own time at Sudeley on this very subject. Last week a new one occurred when we were expecting a plumber to come and deal with an unpleasant situation which had arisen in the children's bathroom. I was buzzed to say that he was here and I opened the door to a gentleman who I showed up to the problem area. After standing there awhile looking rather nonplussed, he asked, 'Is this all there is to see on the tour?' Oh dear – a horrible realisation: the plumber was still waiting at the West Arch and this unhappy fully paid-up visitor, guilty only of waiting at the wrong door to join the Connoisseur Tours, had been shown the wrong exhibit! A happy ending this time as we both had a good laugh, he didn't even ask for a refund and the legitimate plumber managed to sort out the problem. Sudeley must have at least two-dozen doors (I haven't yet counted) which is confusing even to the most initiated.

A high point of this week is the news that we are in the top ten gardens to visit in England in the *Daily Telegraph* listings.

Hooray! And well done to all the gardeners past and present who have helped to get us there.

Ghosts
October 2007

People enjoy exchanging ghost stories and castles are a popular location for such sightings. I have often been asked if Sudeley is haunted and in my day I have heard some strange and curious tales from, guests, visitors and employees alike. In weighing up the evidence and its credibility, I must first confess that over the forty odd years I have been at Sudeley I have never actually come face to face with a ghost. However, having on two occasions had unnerving experiences in other places I have an open mind on the subject and empathy with the Sudeley victims. An encounter with some unexplained apparition or energy can be most alarming and deserves a sympathetic ear.

Reported hauntings at Sudeley range from a dancing stick in the nursery to more than one ashen-faced guest being terrified by a heavy weight sitting on his or her bed in the small hours, items mysteriously tumbling from their perches and other odd occurrences. My sister Genie, not normally susceptible to suggestion and maybe even a ghost sceptic, appeared in my room breathless and emotional (i.e. just short of hysterical) in the small hours of one night saying that a horrid and hostile figure had entered her room and bent threateningly over her bed. He was preceded by a bright light and was dressed in period costume. It took some soothing and a change of bedroom to calm my sister down; to this day she remembers the event vividly.

The most celebrated modern resident ghost is Janet, the formidable and long-serving housekeeper who after retiring to an estate cottage in the early 1950s returned to the castle weekly to make life hell for her successor. After she died Janet continued to spring unexpected visits to the upstairs rooms, running her finger disapprovingly over the furniture and alarming staff and visitors alike. She has been the subject of an article in *Country Life* by Candida Lycett Green and one of the characters depicted in the TV documentary *Haunted Houses of England* made by HRH Prince Edward's production company some years ago. This programme has been repeated often on American and foreign TV and we still have many visitors coming to Sudeley to see where Janet 'lives' as well as the other 'lady', Queen Katherine Parr, who in the series roams the passages and gardens of Sudeley in search of her lost child.

Not only humans are sensitive to spooks and one of my favourite stories of my early married-life at Sudeley involves Muffet and Tessa, the adored and spoilt standard poodles belonging to my late mother-in-law, Mary Dent-Brocklehurst. Suffering from bad breath and overeating, Muffet and Tessa were tolerated but not much loved by the rest of the family. Katie, my sister-in-law, often told a tale of a previous and similar pair of poodles who reportedly on one dark and stormy night following dinner, the family having retired to the drawing room, jumped up and barked and bayed, fur on end, their wild eyes following a passing shadow. Katie was in no doubt that this was the Sudeley ghost.

Later I also became part of the family evening ritual of dining formally and sharply at 8pm and afterwards proceeding to the drawing room where my mother-in-law, flanked by her dogs, would switch on the TV and soon drop off in her chair for a little snooze. On one or two evenings, to lighten up the party, my husband Mark would produce a small water pistol from his pocket and squirt the poodles that would then leap up and race about the room waking their mistress. Mary would say 'Girls, girls, do sit down what has got into you?' After everything had settled down she would return to the TV and soon doze off again until the dogs jumped up once more and rushed around the room waking her up and causing more commotion. By the second or third disturbance Mary would become suspicious and say, 'Mark, are you doing something to upset the dogs?' Mark would look up from his paper and say with convincing innocence, 'No Mummy, it must be the ghost again,' while I stifled giggles behind a book.

These and other ghostly stories continue to enhance our lives at Sudeley. One of my grandchildren recently reported mist floating around his bedroom – coincidentally, the same bedroom with the reported heavy sitting presence. However, since the major renovations undertaken in the 1980s to modernise Sudeley I have not been too worried about staying here alone or walking the corridors at night. The plumbers, electricians, carpenters and decorators saw off the creaking floorboards and draughty passages, the howling air pockets in the Victorian lead pipes, the ill-lit corners and musty damp rooms of my first days at Sudeley. Now the only spectres that seem to remain are the murderous screams of the peacocks at the crack of dawn. However, one soon gets used to them.

Well, you may ask, are there ghosts at Sudeley? I believe that these old stones hold many memories and untold stories, and a few of us, using some unexplained tuning mechanism of our unconscious plus a little imagination, can connect to them. I also know that our sense of humour can have wicked fun with ghouls and spooks and an ancient castle is the ideal place for these musings.

Katherine Parr's Tomb

Katherine Parr, Henry VIII's sixth wife, lived and died at Sudeley, where her life was tranquil and pleasant away from the intrigues of the court. After her death from puerperal fever she was buried not beside the King at Windsor but in the Chapel of St Mary at Sudeley with Lady Jane Grey as Chief Mourner.

Her grave lay undiscovered in the roofless chapel among the Castle ruins until in the summer of 1782 a group of lady sightseers chanced on an alabaster panel attached to one of the Chapel's walls and persuaded Mr Jno Lucas, the tenant farmer, to dig beneath it. To their amazement, not much more than a foot from the surface, he uncovered a leaden coffin, with the inscription 'Here lyeth Quene Kateryn, Wife to Kyng Henry VIII'. He raised the top of the coffin, expecting to discover only the bones of the dead queen, but to his great surprise he found the whole body wrapped in six or seven seer cloths of linen 'entire and uncorrupted', although it had lain there for more than 230 years. His "unwarranted curiosity" also led him to make an incision through the seer cloths into one arm of the corpse which proved to be still white and moist.

This discovery of Katherine Parr's tomb led to more openings of the coffin – both official and mischievous – until 1817 when the then Rector of Sudeley caused it to be removed from the open grave in the ruined chapel into a stone vault of the Chandos family, which was then securely closed. There is a tradition of an ivy berry having fallen into the coffin on one of its openings which had woven itself into a green sepulchral coronet around the dead queen's brow.

Finally in 1861 her leaden coffin was moved into the new tomb in St Mary's Church, beneath the fine Victorian marble effigy designed by George Gilbert Scott and bearing the arms of her four husbands.

Eighteenth century artist's impression of Katherin Parr's coffin.

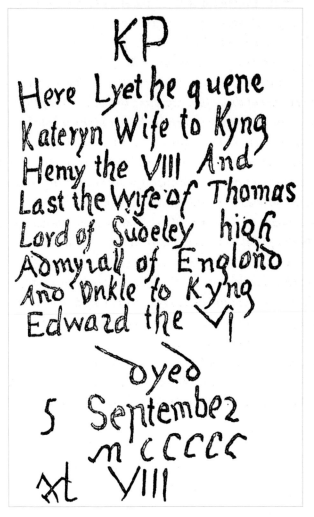

The inscription on the leaden coffin.

Gloucester Street, Winchcombe.

Good Neighbours With Great Character
June 2009

Winchcombe and Sudeley have marched side by side in neighbourly good spirits for over a millennium. Well, perhaps I should say mostly in good spirits as, like all fellow citizens living in close proximity, there are the occasional differences of opinion, inconsideration and other exasperations that tend to ruffle feathers. We are not unlike an old married couple that have put up with each other's annoying habits for so long that we barely bother to comment – unless caught on a bad day.

Emma Dent in her diary entry of 3 May 1879 wrote of a 'long conversation with my housekeeper who told me many discouraging things of the ingratitude of Winchcombe people! I said how I have loved, prayed for, worked for and devoted myself to Winchcombe and did not think there was any love in return'. Obviously, something she had done had miffed the locals and Emma was enjoying a moment of self-pity. She, however, truly did devote her energies, interest and generosity to the community and is kindly remembered to this day for the many benefits she brought to the town.

Sudeley may be splendid and admirable in many ways. However, some may not particularly choose this demanding flamboyant old lady as their ideal next-door neighbour in today's world. For a start, she gives noisy late-night parties and entertainments for boisterous clients, attracts hordes of 'out of towners' and cars through narrow streets, particularly on fine summer days, and could be thought to appear proud and aloof in her grandeur on the edge of the town.

However, despite occasional niggles, I see Winchcombe and Sudeley as great and supportive partners. In simple terms, the thousands of castle visitors bring business to Winchcombe and in turn Winchcombe not only provides Sudeley and the estate with an excellent and up to date back-up of services but its ancient history and charming buildings add appeal and interest to tourists exploring the Cotswolds.

When I first arrived at Sudeley in the early 1960s Winchcombe could be described as a sleepy backwater – an 'interruption' on the road between Cheltenham and Broadway hardly gaining a mention in the guidebooks. I have a hazy memory of George the barber, the butcher, Mrs Mason's popular sweet shop and the George Inn, where our weekend guests often slipped off for a G and T before lunch under the guise of going for a healthy walk. My mother-in-law seemed unaware of the pre-luncheon drink custom that many of our friends enjoyed, although she did produce a silver tray with a bottle of sherry on occasions when entertaining more serious personages for lunch.

Broadway, Chipping Camden, Stow-on-the-Wold and Bourton-on-the-Water were among the picturesque Cotswold villages to explore, maybe stopping to browse in an antique shop, before finding a pub or a hotel dining room for a traditional English meal. Over the years, as tourism became a principle activity in the Cotswolds, these towns have kept up with demands and a burgeoning of B and Bs, quaint shops, souvenir emporiums, country markets, elegant country house hotels, cafés, trendy restaurants and even shopping malls have sprung up on the landscape. But often congested by coaches and sightseers, these lovely towns while catering to popular tastes may have lost a measure of their original character.

Winchcombe on the other hand has retained its genuine ancient quality, while also moving with the times, and providing locals and visitors alike with an impressive list of traditional and sophisticated shops, boutiques, bed and breakfasts, a high-class hotel, restaurants and services. There is neither a souvenir shop nor coach park in sight, and I have become impressed with the quality and variety of the shops and businesses – which could stand up well in a more urban community of worldly clientele.

A great ladies' day out, if you have already visited Sudeley that is, would be to arrive in Winchcombe mid-morning, browse the shops and specialist boutiques, go for a delicious light lunch at one of the many good eateries and wind up with a relaxing beauty treatment in Bull Lane or hair styling in one of Winchcombe's fine hairdressers.

For those with less indulgent and more active interests there are many wonderful walks from the town. My favourite is down Vineyard Street to the river Isbourne and up the old Brockhampton Road to the glorious valley beyond the castle and on to Spoonley Villa to discover its Roman ruins where they lie abandoned in a dense wood. This, of course, is provided you have well and truly exhausted the delights of Sudeley and its magnificent gardens, which out of loyalty to the home team I must encourage you to visit often. It would be difficult to take in all of Sudeley and Winchcombe in one day, so I recommend a two or three day visit.

One of the Sudeley Domesday oak trees.

The Legend of St Kenelm

In 824 King Kenulf of Mercia was succeeded by his seven-year-old son Kenelm much to the chagrin of his elder sister Quendryth who conspired with his tutor Askebert to have him murdered during a hunting trip. Kenelm's body was then buried secretly under a thorn bush at Clent, near Hagley in Worcestershire.

News of the crime was later revealed to Pope Sylvester as he was celebrating Mass in St Peter's in Rome when a white dove flew in through an open window and dropped a parchment scroll on the altar which read: "In Clent cow pasture, under a thorn, of head bereft lies Kenelm, King born."

The Pope instructed that the body should be recovered from Clent and re-buried beside that of his father King Kenulf in Winchcombe Abbey. Monks from Winchcombe set out to search for the body and aided by Kenelm's pet pure white cow his grave was discovered.

When the corpse was disinterred a spring of healing water issued from the spot and as the monks bore it back from Clent to Winchcombe at each stopping place on the journey a spring of water miraculously appeared. The last of these springs, on the Sudeley estate, is known as St Kenelm's Well and in the sixteenth century Sir Thomas Seymour built a conduit house there to supply Sudeley Castle.

Let's Party
September 2008

I find the prospect of guests coming for a short visit a pleasurable one and it usually requires only a little extra effort.

Recently I herded my guests up Sudeley hill to a charming site and monument to the legend of St Kenelm, the murdered boy king, whose corpse is said to have rested there on its way to burial in Winchcombe Abbey – giving rise to a spring of healing water which flows to this day. The conduit house there was built by Sir Thomas Seymour when he owned the castle but records do not reveal if he marched his guests up the mount to take the waters. I doubt if Katherine Parr, Lady Jane Grey or later Queen Elizabeth made the climb, fashion and footwear being as they were at the time, but maybe the young energetic princess Elizabeth was coaxed up the hill by her lusty host and admirer.

Was it fond memories of Seymour I wondered which drew Elizabeth I to keep returning to Sudeley – most memorably for a weekend in September 1592 – which became celebrated as the longest party in history? 'Prior to her arrival Giles 3rd Lord Chandos and his wife Frances Clinton spent months in preparation,' says Emma Dent in her *Annals of Winchcombe and Sudeley* and a poet (probably Gascoigne) was asked to compose verses in the Queen's honour.

Meanwhile the Chandoses prepared the expected emblematic and costly gifts for the queen. Shepherds and shepherdesses, Cotswold sheep and locks of wool were all introduced to the castle to play their part in the pageant. Speeches and holiday clothes were prepared, dogs and bears trained, mummers rehearsed, colours were hoisted and nobility and gentry from far and near assembled. The people were all excitement to see their queen and hoping to participate in the largesse – roasted oxen and ale. Wine for the gentry was contributed by the inhabitants of Tewkesbury who presented Lord Chandos with a hogshead of claret worth £6.

Elizabeth, who had just celebrated her fifty-ninth birthday, rode from Dixton with her mounted escort and the elite of the area escorted by Lord Chandos and was welcomed to Sudeley with a pageant – the prelude to three days of masqueing – bear and bull-baiting, mummers, jousts and feasting, culminating in fireworks, which was then the latest novelty.

The following day, Sunday, there was dancing and an elaborate show was staged. It was the story of Daphne and Apollo, even showing the god pulling out his golden locks and a laurel tree splitting open, out of which Daphne ran to the queen's pavilion 'for whither should Chastity Fly for succour but to the Queen of Chastity'. There were to have been further festivities on the Monday but unfortunately these were rained off and the next day Elizabeth left for Oxford.

What a sight the queen's progresses must have been as they trundled slowly along Cotswold country roads, with hundreds of dignitaries, knights and outriders, not to mention the royal carriage and her 300 plus wagons of personal luggage. And where did they all sleep and what of the other necessary amenities when at Sudeley? It was a relatively small castle even in its original Tudor state and I doubt if there was the variety of bed and breakfasts and pubs that Winchcombe has today.

It must have all been incredibly stressful, not to mention enormously expensive, for the poor Chandos family, and it is astonishing that marriages ever survived Elizabeth I's visits.

I am thinking how lucky I am to be able to host gatherings

at Sudeley some 412 years later when guests' expectations are more modest. One suitcase on wheels will usually suffice, a delicious shepherd's pie or the like with guests often offering to help with the washing up, some good wine, good humour and conversation and the day can be rounded off with a game of Scrabble or the vast choice of entertainment on our new flat screen TV.

The Conduit House at Kenelm's Well.

Superstitions collected from Winchcombe by Emma Dent

If a hare cross your path, it is an evil omen. Better to go back and make a fresh start. To meet a number of pigs is unlucky; but to meet a flock of sheep is a good omen.

If the right eye itches, a surprise awaits you; if the left eye, sorrow. If the right foot itches you have a journey before you. Itching in the right knee – you will soon kneel in a different church.

To make the butter come quickly, dairy maids were advised to stir the cream with a branch of mountain ash and wallop the cows with another branch!

For Cramp. An old Winchcombe woman found relief from nighttime cramp by lying on a poker! Other remedies were to hold a piece of sulphur in one's hand, or to tie around one's leg a band of green periwinkle.

To find the initial of a future lover peel an apple or an orange in one piece and wave it around your head three times. Then gently cast it on the ground. Another sure way was to walk backwards, go to bed backwards and sleep on one's back. Then presumably one dreamt of the lover, initial and all!

The magpie is considered of such evil character that it is supposed to have been the only bird which was not allowed in the ark.

The custom is universal to raise the hat or bow to a magpie, and to say a Paternoster or the alphabet backwards.

October advice (from Celtic folklore): blackberries should not be picked after 11 October, as it was believed that this was when the Devil fell into a thicket of blackberries and cursed the thorns for eternity.

Autumn Past
October 2008

'Echoes fade and memories die; Autumn frosts have slain July.' I do not know the origin of this saying but it seems to match my mood of the moment. Better now to say, 'August rains have slain July' but as it also seems to have rained most of July perhaps this particular quote doesn't quite work. As I write this it is mid-August and it is pouring with rain. My piece for October will be due by the end of next week to meet the publishing deadline and I am trying to think of an October theme with other matters on my mind.

Today we had an in-house meeting to discuss ways of cutting back on our overheads which I'm sure is a subject being discussed and addressed in most homes throughout the land. This spectre conjures up memories of my earliest days at Sudeley, when the old heating system, having been installed by Emma Dent in the late nineteenth century, creaked and groaned up at best a lukewarm radiator with the supplement of an occasional bar on an electric heater. My mother-in-law, proud of her post war austerity and practical philosophy of waste not want not, could sniff out an electric bar left on in one's room from halfway across the castle and pounce like a cat stalking a mouse on the culprit. The culprit was more often than not me as I have never known anything like the agonising, damp, penetrating cold which clung to one's bones and could only be alleviated by getting into a hot bath, or wrapped up with several hot water bottles. Well, that was how it seemed to me at the time.

Over the years I have acclimatised and now actually can't bear over-heated rooms and always sleep with a wide-open window. However, some of the rest of my family seem to be shivering both summer and winter and the half that live most of the year in Hawaii murmur plaintively about the summer weather more often than is necessary, in my opinion. In any case, I think I am doing October an injustice as it usually isn't a very chilly month and can often offer some lovely autumnal days in the garden. I love the russet hues of the changing season and there is nothing more welcoming and warming on a late afternoon than a cup of tea in front of a crackling fire.

Still looking for an October theme, I consulted *Mystical Months*, and quote

A time when the Celtic year, 'Lammas', draws to a close and people prepare for the harshness and impending darkness of 'Samhain', when the circle of the year closes and the sense of death and life is present. A time more than any other when the natural and supernatural are greatly enhanced, with many rituals taking place such as All Hallow's Eve (31 October). The belief in the need to prepare against the closing darker forces was essential. The harsh winter, the darkness, were something to be feared, as not everyone who had enjoyed the summer, sown or harvested, would make it through the long harsh wi...

Oh dear! October is not brightening up as I had hoped. I continue to be in a bleak frame of mind and am running out of words, and the skies are still... But hold on a tick, the sun has just come out again and I hear the cheerful sound of grandchildren and their new puppy romping in the courtyard. I think I will hurry out and join them when I have finished this article.

I apologise for having written such a gloomy review of

October which is really a wonderful month and blameless for the world economic situation, Sudeley in the pre modern heating era and pagan superstitions.

Eighteenth century engraving of Sudeley Castle.

Emma Dent in the Drawing Room, 1890.

Peace In The Parish
November 2008

The stained glass windows and stones of St Mary's, the beautiful little fifteenth-century church in the Sudeley Castle gardens, have been witness to over 600 years of Christian ritual for the people who have lived and worked at Sudeley and in the parish. It has also been ravaged by Oliver Cromwell's armies, abandoned to picturesque ruin and lovingly restored by its nineteenth-century owners, the Dent family. Now gracefully retired to a chapel at ease it still opens its doors for family services, evensong and occasional special celebrations of some of Sudeley's illustrious past inhabitants.

These events are imaginatively created and directed by the present vicar of Winchcombe, John Partington, and are very enjoyable to attend. Recently there was a service to celebrate the life of Queen Katherine Parr on the anniversary of her death 460 years ago. Her remains, after being dug up and re-buried many times, now rest below her most exquisite effigy near the church altar. I had been much looking forward to attending this event until I was unexpectedly delayed with other duties, in the form of my three over-excited grandsons, taking priority. Their parents, who had been in France on a short sun-seeking break, were held up by heavy rain and blocked roads from Bristol and I was still required on 'grandma shift'.

Fortunately the heavens had relented briefly the week before for a very happy family occasion – the christening of my youngest grandchild Jake, an eighteen-month-old cherub-resembling bundle of energy. Parents and grandparents, godparents and a few friends, plus a handful of children gathered in the church where we took part in a charming, heart warming and child friendly service devised and lead by the resourceful Reverend Partington. The children hopped, sang and clapped to favourite hymns and songs and the parents behaved like demented paparazzi taking photographs. Jake, the guest of honour, stomped and sang along and let out a loud chuckle when lifted at the font for the Baptism. I don't know what this means for his character but we will hope for the best.

The relationship between Emma Dent, the Victorian chatelaine of Sudeley, and her spiritual leader, the Reverend Noble Jackson, was not so convivial according to Emma in her diaries. Jean Bray's delightful book *The Lady of Sudeley* tells us of dark days in the parish.

This was an era of passionate religious controversy where differences of style could lead to fierce antagonism. Mr Jackson, formally a friend and the curate of St Mary's, when promoted to vicar of Winchcombe appointed a ritualist to take his place as the new curate of Sudeley. John Dent, Emma's husband, was incensed, complained to the Bishop about this 'Romanism' on his doorstop and asked for his removal.

Emma exacerbated the situation by directing that Catechism should be dispensed with at the local King's School. On hearing of this the Reverend Jackson lost his head and became very abusive. More insults and outrages ensued, culminating in the vicar refusing to say the burial service correctly over people he disliked or disapproved of (including John Dent) and the feud between the former friends was to run for the rest of their lives. Even the *Cheltenham Examiner* reported on the unfolding story.

Emma bitterly quotes 'How incredible it seems that a man of 50 should retain such uncharitable and cruel views. Poor Rev'd

Noble Jackson – I am sorry to say he is another example of the uncertainly of men having been admirable in one position being unable to bear a promotion to power.' Records do not reveal what the reverend may have said about Emma!

Fortunately today the parish of Winchcombe and Sudeley seems at peace with itself. Our kind and versatile vicar of both churches and several more in the vicinity is able to devise ceremonies to suit all tastes and leanings and the *Gloucestershire Echo* doesn't seem to be the least bit concerned. How lucky we are.

The Lady of Sudeley is on sale at Sudeley Castle and all bookshops and I can highly recommend it to anyone who would enjoy an intimate insight into the life and secret thoughts of an extraordinary Victorian woman.

In the winter of 1928-29 there was a severe frost – three nights of 30 degrees frost. The moat at Sudeley was frozen with ice inches thick and the local 'upper ten' came to skate. When the skaters went home to lunch we took new besoms and swept the ice for them. The ladies and gents rewarded us with half crowns and that made the week even more golden for us.

Bert Butler was an under-gardener at Sudeley in the 1920s and this is an extract from his book Cotswold Ragbag.

Winter

Memories Of Christmas Past
December 2007

Eating roast beef and plum pudding with old faces – joining in a merry dance and still more merry games at cards – and warbling and waltzing on uncarpeted boards until 2 o'clock in the morning.

These festive words have travelled over time by way of my great-great aunt Emma's diaries, which have been an invaluable resource and source of inspiration to me over the years.

Emma Dent was the spirited and indefatigable Victorian chatelaine of Sudeley whose influence still pervades our daily lives and whose shoes I have sometimes found it challenging to fill. The following extracts from her diaries tell that familiar tale of 'Yuletide' that we all recognise so well: families, feasting, parties, games, presents, reflection, nostalgia... and the weather!

1859: On Christmas Eve we had my Fife and Drum Band at the Castle, they played all their best and most military tunes, ending with the *Roast Beef of Old England*, then they marched into the Hall and the 18 Fifers, 4 drums and 2 triangles were regaled with as much roast beef and plum pudding as they could eat.

Christmas Day – and we dined alone for the first time since our marriage in 1847, having always spent our Christmas Days with the Uncles in Worcester while they were living and then with

Uncle William at Titherington – but they are all gone – what changes pass over families in a few short years.

On the 26th the servants had a party, consisting of husbands, wives and children, Marianne and I for their amusement dressed up – she in the Bear's Dress and I as Old Christmas – we made our appearances on the balcony of the servants hall and were greeted with thundering applause – we lowered Christmas presents amongst them and disappeared as we appeared.

1861: I had my German tree ready – and all the cottagers and their children came to see it in the drawing room – it was a very pretty sight to see all the astonished children standing around. [German tree because the tradition of decorated Christmas trees was introduced by Prince Albert.]

1880: Christmas. A sad letter from Uncle William, he feels isolated compared to what it was 30 or 40 years ago when we were a large and united family and our elders still in the front! The ties seem to be loosening every year more and more as Xmas comes round, the ground loosening under our feet –as if preparing to receive us! Ah well – we must all take life as we find it – try to do no harm, as much good as we can, work as hard as we can…

We have had all our cottagers to tea and given them petticoats and presents – with others including cottagers, making up about 100 presents has made me very busy.

1886: Very deep snow, roads almost impassable, footpaths invisible – fly and pair brought me home from the station. Snow frozen on the trees and shrubs – obliged to postpone three days shooting.

1887 – Deep snow as last year, but having had hot water (central heating) introduced into the Castle (just in time) it makes the cold bearable. Today very severe outside. I saw five partridges and a multitude of field hares helping themselves to the food put for the birds just outside the study window on a patch of green swept clear of the snow.

1891 Jan 1: The frost has now lasted three weeks, skaters on the moat, morning noon and night – it all looks very bright and cheery, especially at night either by torch or moonlight.

1894: Snow fell – wind bringing great drifts. By daylight five men were on the roof of the Castle, for four hours they were clearing if off the roof. In Winchcombe people were literally snowed up, Church empty, everybody working at their own doors… thaw set in – a good deal of damage was done to the stonework by the expanding of the ice.

1895: Carol singers came into the quadrangle and sang, very picturesque they looked with their lanterns shining on the snow.

Well, many changes have taken place at Sudeley over the past 150 years. No more presents and entertainment for 100 cottagers; roast beef has been superseded by the ubiquitous turkey (no doubt the influence of my country of birth), the fly and pair sadly no longer reside in the stables (now home to our Emma Dent exhibition), but one thing that does remain constant is that ever-perplexing topic of the weather!

Instead of couching out in front of the telly after an over indulgent Christmas dinner, wouldn't it be lovely to pick up one's skates and head down to the frozen lake for a bracing glide?

Christmas at Sudeley, 1962.

Left: Mr Whittle with the cook and other staff. *Right*: Nanny Ewins.

By 7am the Kitchen staff and the Pantry staff will be doing their respective jobs. The kitchen range is never out. It was started by smokeless fuel and the staff have to cook and prepare porridge and main dish for 1. the Nursery and 2. the Servants.

The Pantry staff also start at 7am. The Footman puts his apron on in the Pantry and goes up to the Dining room with a tray of all that is necessary for the Major's breakfast. He will also prepare a Tray for Mrs D.B. and leave it in the kitchen. The Butler, wearing a dark suit, white shirt, stiff collar and looking dignified looks around the ground floor. If the Major has been sharing the bed with the Mrs. he does not go in, but the ladies maid can go in, remembering to knock and wait. If the Major is using his room near then the Butler will come in and put a light on and pull the curtains... The Major may ask about the weather. The Butler may look out and comment briefly on the weather, as far as he could.

The Hall Boy – me – goes into the Pantry, takes off my jacket and puts a dark apron on. I go into the Servants Hall, take duster and brush the table, put the tablecloth on and lay the table remembering, sugar, salt and pepper etc. At 7.50am I go to the Kitchen with a tray and take the food for the Hall. I then ring the handbell for the breakfast.

Extract from Mr Whittle's letters to Elizabeth Ashcombe.

Upstairs Downstairs
January 2008

One might imagine that the winter months at Sudeley when the castle is closed to visitors would bring a welcome respite, a time for other interests and not much going on. Alas, this is not the case; it is our busiest time of year.

Planning for next season's events, major house and garden maintenance and serious housekeeping gets underway. These jobs are carried out by a small and dedicated staff with the help of modern equipment. Even so, we rarely complete these labours in time and there is usually a frenzied rush in early March for the countdown to the spring opening.

Another winter project, which is sadly lagging behind, is my book, a memoir and archive of twentieth-century life at Sudeley. I have been reviewing my notes, letters and conversations over time with the many people who have helped me put this fascinating story together. Luckily there were a few who remembered Sudeley in the earlier part of this century. One in particular, and a gift dropped from heaven, was John Whittle, who came to the castle as hall boy in 1930, and who revisited Sudeley in his retirement and began a long correspondence with me. His amazing observation and memory for detail are a delight and a great insight into an era when the maintenance and domestic running of the castle was still in the hands of a large number of people looking after the comforts of a very few, in a manner reminiscent of *Upstairs Downstairs*.

Early in Nov. 1930 the Major (Jack Dent-Brocklehurst) sent a
card to my father telling him that he would start me on Monday
1st December. At 10am Mr. Pearce, the chauffeur came to collect
me at Elms Farm, Teddington. My father seemed glad to get rid
of me. He had listened to me talking about the crash of Wall
Street and other matters and he said, 'all this book learning will
not do thee any good'.

Edward (under butler) showed me to my bedroom over the
boiler on the first floor. There were two beds – the second one
was for visiting chauffeurs. My bed was near the window and I
could see Cleeve Hill. For the first time in my life I was able to go
to bed on my own and when a chauffeur came for a few days I
enjoyed their chat! I had a bed with white sheets and pillowslips,
two blankets and an overleaf. 1 chest of drawers, 1 wardrobe,
1 mat, 2 chairs, 1 chamber pot – white. The room had brown
linoleum and nice curtains. Everything in the room was clean
and wholesome. For one night, at least, I felt like a Prince.

At 12 noon on Monday I had my first meal in the Servants
Hall. All there were Mr. Buckingham – the Butler, Janet – the
Head House maid, Cook, the Footman, Odd man, Kitchen Maid,
Scullery Maid, Lady's Maid, Janet's 2nd, 3rd and 4th housemaids,
Mr. Pearce – the Chauffeur, Maud – the laundress and her 2
Maids and me, the Hall boy. In the children's part was Nanny
Ewins and the assistant nanny. There was also a Governess but I
am sure that you know they are above the hoi polloi of common
servants, yet below the Gentry! Outside staff were Mr. Pearce
– head Gardener plus his staff of six. There was always an Estate
Manager and a few workers working on the Estate but I am not
sure on that matter.

John Whittle died in 2005, aged eighty-nine. After leaving
service at Sudeley he went on to rise among the ranks to become
under-butler to Lady Astor. What a delight it was to have
known him and the many colourful household characters who
he brought back to life.

Upstairs Downstairs Redux

I couldn't write about Mr Whittle or other past household employees without mentioning something about our own dear John Gilpen, the last Sudeley butler, when we still had such luxuries. John was a character, feared by some, loved by others. I always had a soft spot for him, having learned my way around his fiery temper and wily ways. When a guest of any distinction came to stay or for a meal, he could bow, scrape, M'Lord and M'lady, with the best of them, but to others his style tended to be a little more brusque. Thinking I was out of ear shot, I once heard him shouting 'Knickers' out of the pantry window at Mrs. Marshall, our excellent but very straight laced housekeeper. He was of portly bearing and made a most convincing Father Christmas, thrilling my children and their cousins when he crept across the courtyard on Christmas Eve with a black sack slung over his back. John's passion was playing the drums in a brass band, and when a parade beckoned, his loyalty to the band took precedent over any duties at Sudeley. Family and friends alike have plenty of anecdotes to illustrate their fond memories of John, but none made quite so public as the following....

A few years ago I was alerted to an article, which appeared in the *Sunday Mail*, written by Tom Utley. I remembered Tom well as the nice young man who came to tutor my son for his forthcoming exams. I had been impressed over the years to see his name rising through the ranks to become a successful and well-known journalist. Reading the article I was horrified to learn that Tom had been subjected to such an uncomfortable stay at Sudeley and immediately wrote to him with my very belated apologies. I had a letter by return to say he hoped I hadn't taken it the wrong way and that he had used a little licence to make it a good story. I have taken an excerpt from the longer article, which goes on to write about why Brits make bad servants concluding 'we have too much pride and sense of our own self worth to put our hearts into waiting on others.'

Only once have I stayed in a house that had a full Upstairs-Downstairs complement of live-in servants, butler and all.

This was Sudeley Castle in Gloustershire, where I was employed in the mid 1970s as a tutor to the young Henry Dent-Brocklehurst, who was coming up for his Common Entrance Exam. I was just down from Cambridge.

I meant to write a book about my experiences, but as with every other masterpiece I've conceived over the past 30 years, I never got beyond the title. This one was to be a dazzlingly witty and perceptive analysis of the British class system, and it was to be called 'Halfway up the Stairs'.

I was proud of that title, because it neatly summed up my position at the castle. I ate with the family – except when Henry's widowed mother (now Lady Ashcombe) had guests. Then I was consigned to the servants' hall. It was all rather awkward. I was terrified of the butler, a fellow Englishman, who never let me forget that I was a mere employee, just like him. He made it clear he resented having to wait on me when I was eating with the family. I would probably have felt the same in his shoes.

Worse, Mrs D-B had told me that if ever I wanted a cup of tea or coffee, I should just ring the bell. I tried it once, though I didn't feel happy about it. I was perfectly capable of making my own coffee – and I knew the butler's feelings about serving this 22 year-old, middle-class squit with the long hair, the M&S cords and the desert boots.

After I'd timidly placed my order, he stomped into the room where I was teaching Henry and slammed the coffee tray down in front of me, with a look so venomous that I never dared ask him for anything again.

Matters came to a head one morning when he caught me sneaking into the kitchen, between Henry's lessons, to put the kettle on for myself. 'That's my job', he snapped – and I retreated to the school room where, a few minutes later, he went through the tray slamming, venomous-look routine for the second and last time.

I couldn't win: not allowed to ask, not allowed to make my own. From then on, no more morning coffee for me. So I spent my whole time at Sudeley in a state of exquisite middle class angst, desperately wishing there were no servants around....

Tom Utley, the Sunday Mail, July 27, 2007

Left: John Gilpen. *Right*: Mr Whittle.

RUINS OF SUDELEY CASTLE.

Sudeley Ruins

The ruins of Sudeley had lain neglected and left to the ravages of the weather until it was rescued in the nineteenth century by John and William Dent, wealthy glovemakers from Worcester.

The Dents were enthusiastic antiquarians on the look-out for an interesting project on which to spend their considerable fortune when riding in the Cotswold hills they saw the ruined Castle and estate spread out below them and determined to acquire it. Lord Rivers who had already put the estate on the market agreed to sell it to them in 1830 but they had to wait another seven years before they were able to buy the Castle itself and the remaining 60 acres from the Duke of Buckingham and Chandos. Finally in 1837 Sudeley Castle and estates were united by the Dents and by 1840 a large part of the building was habitable once again.

Growing Old
February 2008

I recently revisited a book that a friend of mine, Susanna Johnston, had asked me to contribute to *LATE YOUTH: An Anthology of the Joys of Being Over Fifty*.

More than 100 talented, dynamic, and for the most part famous, friends of Susanna's contributed a wealth of wit, wisdom and poignant reading on this inevitable condition. I find my own piece dullish in comparison to the musings of such literary luminaries as Melvyn Bragg, Jilly Cooper and Patrick Leigh Fermor, or celebrities like Dame Edna Everage, and would prefer to delight the readers of this column with quotes from their entries. However, I will stick to my brief to talk about life at Sudeley Castle, which is something that, at least, I feel qualified to do.

Getting older and sharing aches and pains with an ancient building is a challenging way to pass one's later days. After more than forty years one gets to know the little foibles and idiosyncrasies of the crumbling stones. Having suffered the ravages of war and neglect over the centuries Sudeley responds well, as we all do, to a little understanding and tender loving care. She doesn't like being too hot or too cold, or too wet or too dry, and she reacts petulantly when conditions are not comfortable. Damp causes the stone to sweat, moulds such as the deadly dry rot can appear and paint flakes. Dry causes major environmental concern, dust which rots valuable textiles and parches the garden causing some of our beautiful plants to die. Heat causes the beams to expand and make spooky noises and cold contracts them again, with worrying consequences for oil paintings and fine furniture. Water is the most threatening element and we are just getting to grips with the damage done in the summer floods which so severely hit this part of the country.

Looking after a large, quirky fifteenth-century building, susceptible to the ravages of all the above and more is a demanding job for all of us who work here. However, we tackle it with loving dedication and gently try to coax our patient back into good shape. Sudeley has fascinated, challenged, maddened, and at times almost driven me batty but nevertheless I love the place and I am constantly trying to think of new ways and medicines to improve 'the old lady's' ageing issues.

This certainly helps to keep my mind off my own but this time of year, following the excesses of the festive season, hints that a little extra personal maintenance wouldn't go amiss. Detox is not a pretty word and the drinks and potions that accompany it certainly do not have an appetising appeal. The little used exercise machine has been hauled out of retirement, and most of my favourite foods are off the menu. To keep my mind off this tiresome regime my imagination heads to the garden and spring and those far off unimaginable warm days of summer. Sudeley is at its most enchanting in late spring and early summer when the skies are blue, the hues of colours seduce the eye, the heady scented flowers finally reappear after their long incubation and the castle again looks content in the beauty of its surroundings. It is well worth waiting for I'm telling myself on this dark, damp and dreary evening, and in the meantime I dream, plan and wait, and am grateful to have been given the opportunity to help make and shape this small but unique corner of the world.

'If these stones could talk', it has often been said, and how could one mind growing old with such a fascinating companion who has housed and entertained so many great and celebrated figures of the past while bearing witness to some of the most intriguing times of English history? Sudeley will certainly survive me and mine, as it has all its previous owners, but I hope to continue to be part of its story for a while to come.

Queen Mary with the Dent-Brocklehurst family in 1944.

Oliver Cromwell is reputed to have cancelled Christmas – in fact the Puritans did attempt to cancel it for a time to prevent its celebration with drunkenness and gluttony. At Sudeley, Cromwell is remembered for 'slighting' the Castle at the end of the Civil War during which it played a strategic role – serving in turn as both a Royalist stronghold and a Parliamentary garrison. While in Royalist hands it came under siege twice and a hole in the Octagon Tower which can still be seen was blown by a fusillade of cannon fire during the final battle.

In 1649 the Council of State ordered that the castle be 'slighted' or made untenable as a military post which involved removing the roof and exposing the entire building to the weather. Sudeley was effectively demolished in August and September of that year, much of it never to be built again.

Time For A Change
December 2008

This is the time of year for our traditional thinking, planning and shopping for the forthcoming 'festive' season. The time to anticipate the long – in my opinion too long – over-indulgent, build-up of frenzy to celebrate our material culture, which is now going through a great metamorphosis.

We cannot turn a corner or even a page without being faced with the credit crunch, bankruptcies and job losses, and doom and gloom is being forecast by the media across the board. Although alarming and uncertain on so many levels, could it be that this global economic and environmental crisis is offering us a chance to re-evaluate our priorities and regain a sense of true value in our lives?

We are being frog-marched to recognise that collectively we are using too much water and energy, wasting too much food, travelling too much, having too many gadgets, clothes and things – most of which we don't need and bring us little real satisfaction – not to mention the unforgivable inequality of the distribution of life sustaining resources to much of the world's people. Being aware of these facts is an opportunity we all have, but how to manage them on a personal level is more perplexing.

We at Sudeley Castle, like so many others, are struggling to think what our options are if there is to be a dramatic downturn in our business in the foreseeable future, even though our visitor numbers have seen an increase of 34 per cent this season. The preservation of the historic buildings at Sudeley and the conservation of the contents are dependent on our paying visitors and their continued patronage and enjoyment of the gardens and exhibitions. Will family outings and general tourism be affected by the credit crunch? I expect that they will. Can we cut down on our overheads? I don't know that we can by very much without detriment to the very object that we have set out to preserve.

However, I believe that Sudeley is a place where many people come to feed their spirit, to breathe in the timeless beauty of its surroundings, to take some time off from their daily lives and concerns and step into another era when technology and self gratification were not the priority.

All through the ages people have struggled with the problems and upheavals of their times and creative and imaginative people have sought solutions for them. England's unique wealth of architecture, historic houses, gardens, museums and galleries are not selling the trivial and disposable products of our materialistic culture, but bear witness to something more tangible, valuable and perhaps set an example to learn from in times of crisis.

I have felt fortunate to have been custodian of Sudeley's heritage over almost forty years, but saddened to watch our visitor numbers drop off to our competitors – shopping malls, theme parks, Sunday shopping, cheap foreign travel and the like. It has been suggested that we are rather an old fashioned attraction; we need to be more cutting edge, use interactive technology, to create new excitement every year to attract new interest. Well, quite frankly, this is exhausting even to think about, let alone to achieve. I wonder if at Sudeley and other similar historic houses there may be an opportunity in the light of the present cultural revolution for the revival of our traditional role as an accessible repository of some of our country's rich history and heritage.

Returning to my Christmas theme, I remember a scene played out under our Christmas tree last year, when after the hysteria of tearing open and chucking aside the piles of presents from well meaning parents, grandparents, godparents and Father Christmas, my grandchildren were having a tremendous game of pulling each other around in one of the large boxes that had packaged an expensive remote control toy. Later the box was turned into a house where the air conditioning system was demonstrated by flapping the cardboard folds back and forth. I think the competition for the box ultimately turned to tears and bed and bath time were promptly announced as emergency measures, but nevertheless 'out of the mouths of babes'...

Hmmm, I'm wondering if I can get away with cardboard boxes this Christmas, and I am hoping that Sudeley can get away with just plain old fashioned humdrum Henry VIII and his wives, prize winning gardens, and an impressive collection of historical and artistic treasures to soothe the senses of our hard pressed customers next season.

Mark and Elizabeth on their wedding day, with Alfie.

First Impressions
January 200

January ... out with the old, in with the new – a time to celebrate the birth of new opportunities, and make new resolutions for better health and wealth – a time to meet friends and remember old friends, a time for reflection and hope.

It is also on record as the coldest month of the year. I'm sorry to immediately reflect on January's worst aspect, but it is difficult to be cheery and positive, loving and resolute, when one is constantly preoccupied with draughts and burst pipes, stoking the fire, searching for warm gloves, trying to conserve on heating, not managing very well and pining away in the long dark evenings.

My first ever sight of Sudeley was sometime in mid-January back in the dark ages of the early sixties, when I, a young design student in New York, came over to visit England at the invitation of my then unsuspecting husband-to-be, Mark Brocklehurst. He had met my plane in Paris where we had a merry whirl around that exciting and romantic city, and returned to London for the week where he deposited me in a small hotel, and went to work as usual leaving me to explore London for the first time. He had told me little of Sudeley Castle, except that it was his family home and that we would go there for the weekend where I would meet his mother. By now I had heard a lot about his castle in Gloucestershire and particularly about his mother who was described colourfully by his friends and I suspected a somewhat intimidating experience was in store for me. I was nervous, but Mark jollied me along and said 'Oh you'll be fine, the old girl's not as bad as all that'.

Mark was devoted to his whippet Alfie who I also took to right away, and we three set off for Sudeley. The drive from London, before motorways, took longer than it does now and it was Mark's habit to leave London around 6pm, drive to Marlow-on-Thames, have dinner at the Compleat Angler and then another couple of hours on the road until we finally turned into the Castle gates.

It was a misty night and my first sight of my future home was in the dark with the Castle's towers, castellation, trees and ruins outlined in the ghostly moonlight. Before I could take a breath Mark let Alfie out of the backseat where he promptly leapt onto the lawn, chasing rabbits, with Mark in hot pursuit using the car's headlights. This seemed to be a regular joy ride when reaching their Friday night destination. With Alfie well exercised we parked the car, unloaded the suitcases and proceeded along what seemed like miles of dimly lit passages until we reached the icy cold Lace Bedroom where I was to sleep, with instructions that he would meet me in the dining room the next morning at 8.30 am sharp ... and dressed?

I remember getting up the next morning and the water in my basin had frozen over. I switched on the one functioning electric bar on my radiator and shivering 'dressed' as instructed, choosing my smart red channel style suit with gold buttons which I guessed Mark might think suitable for my first meeting with his mother. With high heels, makeup, and hair brushed I set off to find the dining room... and Mark. His mother was already there, in country tweeds and sensible shoes with thick warm stockings, but there was no sign of Mark. I was a bag of nerves. She was very gracious and courteous, asking the how was your trip over and how did you leave the weather in New York sort of questions. Brown, the Butler, a dear fellow, small like a gnome complete with a mole on his nose, appeared with a sumptuous cooked breakfast – bacon, fried eggs, sausages, tomatoes ... the lot, and put it on the sideboard. I helped myself to all and coffee and still very nervous sat down at the table where to the side of me was a pretty little silver pot with what I assumed to be brown sugar in it. I stirred a spoonful into my coffee but the brown sugar wouldn't melt, it all floated to the top. I drank the coffee, still having the polite conversation with Mrs D-B but now the 'sugar' was stuck around my lips and to the roof of my mouth. It turned out that the little silver pot held not brown sugar at all but her wheat germ that she put on her cereal. Twigging that it wasn't sugar I tried to discretely lick it off when she wasn't looking. Neither of us said anything. Mark finally appeared at around 9:30 in his dressing gown to his mother's rather testy greeting, 'Mark dear you've kept Brown waiting to clear breakfast and I see you've been driving on the lawn again.' He winked, rolled back his eyes, and said ingenuously, 'Sorry Mummy'. I would soon learn that 'Sorry Mummy' was his only concession to an apology no matter what offence had been done.

Later, he told me she'd said to him 'Elizabeth is very smart, isn't she', no doubt inferring that I was over dressed for breakfast. The next morning Brown put a tiny little silver bowl of wheat germ next to my coffee. Obviously they both thought it was an odd American custom to put wheat germ in the coffee and I felt obliged to carry on with the charade the following morning.

Had I thought then that I would one day come to live in this eccentric cold spooky mausoleum, I would have bolted on the spot. Fate decided otherwise and here I am today looking forward to my forty-seventh January with our comfortable now central-heated rooms; cosy fires and most mod cons... with fingers crossed against frozen pipes and blocked gutters.

Elizabeth with Henry (three) and Mollie (infant).
(*Inset*) Brocklehurst family crest.

Brock

This is an article that I had wanted to include in Cotswold Life but I couldn't find the heart to reduce it to the agreed length. I am delighted to have the opportunity to include it in these pages.

It makes me feel sad when these days I see so many dead badgers on the side of the road. The badger has got a bad reputation among farmers. Whether this is entirely justified or not is a question in dispute on which I am unable to comment with any knowledge. I can, however, speak up for the fascinating, intelligent, wily, teasing and loving character of one particular badger, our old pet Brock. This tale goes back many years when my now middle-aged offspring were young and we were living in London, but on the threshold of taking up our new life at Sudeley. The year was 1969.

When at Sudeley on weekends my husband Mark had a habit of slipping off to Evesham to meet his 'dealer', a rough-hewn sort who dealt in all sort of unusual and exotic birds and small animals, sometimes of questionable origin. I usually declined to go on these expeditions due to my aversion to snakes like a free roaming boa constrictor but it was Mark's idea of heaven to have a good chinwag with this type as he was laying down the foundations of his bird and pheasant collection. This later grew into a major visitor attraction at Sudeley.

Mark's great love of wildlife didn't preclude him from keeping some of his collection in our house in Kensington which we shared with a menagerie of three dogs, a mynah bird, a bad tempered cockatoo (the latter two acquired from the above source) and two children. The mynah bird had a vocabulary limited to 'B...r off!' cackling and coughing. We didn't know who his previous owner was, but Mark guessed it was a bad debt settled with the dealer. Maureen, our treasured nanny, was none too impressed with the birds' language, and the conservatory, where they lodged in sumptuous comfort, was off limits to Henry and Mollie.

One weekend, the children and I having stayed in London, Mark returned late Sunday night and woke me with unusual scuffling and excitement saying, 'darling, come and see what I have brought you'. He was struggling up the stairs with an ungainly and strange smelling crate that opened to reveal two small, furry and hungry black and white creatures tucked up in a towel. We crept into the nursery kitchen, did the necessary and tucked them up snug again for the night. I said to Mark, 'we can't leave them here. Maureen will have a fit'. So they slept in our bathroom with several more demands for feeds throughout the night.

I don't remember being wholly enthusiastic about the surprise but Mark reassured me – one badger would go to his mother and the remaining one 'would be no trouble at all'. The next morning Mark went to the office and left me to deal with the situation. Without further ado I picked up the crate, now in need of an urgent clean, and took it to the nursery hoping the resourceful Maureen would take charge. Unfortunately, her reaction was not as positive as I would have hoped and after one look she did a full swivel and with hands on hips said, 'Either those filthy animals leave my nursery, or I do!' It annoyed Mark if I rang him at the office on a minor pretext but I thought this seemed quite major as after two or three unsuccessful starts in the nanny department, I wasn't prepared to gamble with Maureen. Mark gave short shrift to my panic call and said, 'Tell her to calm down and I'll take them back to the country on Friday'.

After a token huff and puff, Maureen got down to the business of feeds and bedding changes and by Friday she had bonded with the two cubs and decided we should keep the female. Brock from then on was treated as a member of the family but for some reason was always referred to as 'he'. True to his word, Mark deposited the other little fellow with his mother, recently installed in her new house, Hawling Manor, where as 'Badgie' he resided in a comfortable kennel and was lovingly spoiled.

Brock thrived under Maureen's expert care and was soon in the full swing of nursery routine. Brock was bottle fed with an occasional comforting suckle at Maureen's ear. 'Oh you daft thing,' she would say feigning annoyance.

Badgers are clean and hygienic animals in the wild and do not soil their set. As Brock matured he too refused to do his business in the house and found for himself a suitable drain in the garden over which he would squat; afterwards to be hosed down.

The four – Henry on foot, Mollie and Brock in the pushchair and Maureen in charge – would set off for the park on fine days where they would join the gaggle of other nannies and their charges. There was an exclusive area in Kensington Gardens where only crested prams and titled nannies dare venture. Maureen was occasionally invited into this lofty circle due to the fact that our cousin's nanny was a terrific snob and had a royal nanny connection. I asked her once what the other nannies made of Brock and she said after the first meeting or so they treated him like any other of their charges – 'my hasn't he grown' or 'looking smart' or some such comment before getting down to the real gossip of the day.

As Brock grew he graduated from the pushchair to walking behind on a lead and was quite a traffic stopper. He soon became frisky but would get a proper telling off and clip around the ears from Maureen if he got too rumbunctious. He enjoyed such skittish pranks as hiding behind a curtain or chair lying in wait for an unsuspecting pair of ankles to pass by for a playful pounce. As he was soon the size of a small bear with a full set of sparkling sharp teeth, thanks to strict dental care rules in the nursery, the joke was not so amusing to those, including myself, who were starting to become wary of his fiendish sense of humour. The truth was that Brock didn't really care much for humans other than Mark, Mollie and Maureen. They were his family and anyone else was an outsider. For some reason Henry had fallen foul due to teasing and I was never part of his inner circle. Even our whippets gave him a wide birth and refused to sit in the back seat with him on our weekly trips to Sudeley.

Brock by now was starting to show his native instincts by sleeping most of the day under the bed and then around teatime livening up for nocturnal fun and adventure. He moved downstairs and a cat flap was installed so that he could slip out for an evening ramble around our garden. One morning we discovered he had failed to return and a great search was mounted. The children, Maureen and I looked everywhere and Mark was on standby for news at the office. His disappearance was reported to the police and later an officer appeared at the door to say that an address in the next street had reported a wild animal in their garden and that the RSPCA had been alerted.

We all rushed around to the house where the bemused and ashen-faced owners showed us to the top of a winding wrought iron staircase and pointed towards the bottom of their garden. A rustle in the shrubbery and out shot Brock lumbering at top speed across the grass, up the winding staircase, and flinging himself into Maureen's capacious outstretched arms, he started to suckle her ear. 'Oh you daft thing,' she said, 'what a lot of fuss you've caused.' Poor Brock was as upset as we were and as the RSPCA van arrived with their nets he was seen being carried away while I was left to apologise to the owners for all the holes and mess in their garden and promise to make reparations.

We soon discovered that Brock had been digging in other well-tended gardens up and down the road. It was time for him to move to the country. To start with he wasn't that keen on life at the castle, particularly because he couldn't find his old drain. He soon solved this problem by discovering the plughole in the bath next to the Campaign room, which was also our primary guest bathroom and to this day it is still known as the Badger Bathroom. Sharing intimate space with a badger is not most people's idea of country house hospitality and after several embarrassing quick hose downs and apologies to our wrinkled nosed guests, plus, the last straw, tangling himself up in the seventeenth-century lace bed-hangings on view to the public and shocking our visitors, Brock was invited to kindly take up lodging in the kennels.

He was a handsome specimen with luxurious coat and bright eyes, much photographed by his doting owner, and sat for his portrait by well-known animal painter, Neil Foster. Neil later told me he was a difficult subject and he'd had to chase him all around the courtyard trying to capture a good likeness while at the same time avoiding those intimidating jaws.

Brock by now was enormous; only Mark could pick him up. He slept in the kennel all day and was taking his nightly missions more seriously. Once or twice he didn't come back for two days or so. Then, inevitably, one sad time he never came back.

We told Mollie that 'she' had probably met a nice fellow and decided to set up home with him. Recently a well-known biologist and friend of mine asked Mollie what it was like to share her pram and nursery table with a badger. She thought for a minute and said, 'It seemed perfectly natural to me. No one suggested otherwise'.

Above: 2. The topiary figures represent Katherine Parr and Lady Jane Grey on their path to St Mary's church.

Left: 3. The Tithe Barn.

4. The Tithe Barn Garden.

Above: 7. The Queen's Garden.

Right: 8. Mary Dent-Brocklehurst, first woman High Sheriff of Gloucestershire 1967.

Opposite page: 6. St Mary's Church.

10. Mark with Brock.

11. Mollie and Brock.

12. The Sheldon Tapestry.

Opposite page:
9. Left to right: Violet Ward, Jake Brocklehurst, Mark Brocklehurst, Lucien Ward, Luca Brocklehurst, Christmas 2008.

Above: 14. Duncan, Mollie and Lucien Ward, 2002.

Opposite page: 13. Henry and Lili, 1998.

15. The Library.

16. Elizabeth and Zabik.

19. Chandos Bedroom.

Above: 20. Elizabeth and Henry receiving the Garden of the Year Award, 1996.

Right: 21. Lord Ashcombe.

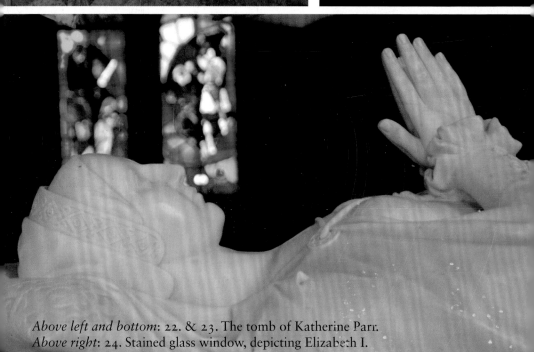

Above left and bottom: 22. & 23. The tomb of Katherine Parr.
Above right: 24. Stained glass window, depicting Elizabeth I.

A Month For Lovers
February 2009

Is February a month to be avoided if at all possible, or should it be a great moment to knuckle down and plan for sunnier days? It is hard to avoid, as it arrives inevitably after a trying January and sticks around for four weeks before introducing us to what is usually a blustery, cold and wet March.

The readers of this column will now realise from this barrage of grumbling, that I am not a skier, I do not hunt, follow the hounds, revel in going out with the guns to watch a pheasant slaughter, or enjoy any of the pursuits that many sensible country people have devised to take their minds off this dreary time of year. In my early life in America the winter provided beautiful scenes with fallen snow and frozen lakes for sledging, skating, snowman building and the like and all the trimmings that went with them. At least that is how I remember it.

At Sudeley now we seldom see the castle covered in snow described by Emma Dent in Victorian times as 'looking like a wedding cake'.

Despite this, February has a special appeal for romantics and lovers with Valentine's Day to anticipate, and it is around this time of year that many brides-to-be start dreaming of a fairy-tale spring or summer wedding. We are delighted that Sudeley has again won the Wedding Venue of the Year award, and over the years we have received many wonderful and rewarding letters and accolades from brides and their families about their special day here. The backdrop of the castle provides an enchanting setting for the occasion and I often peep out of my window to see a bride arriving in a coach and four... a scene right out of Jane Austen.

However, in February, with fewer brides and romantic views from my window, I try and go to warmer, more exotic lands to escape the winter blues. For the past three years I have joined a group of friends in Goa where we share a wonderful, sprawling house on the beach with not much to do but swim, laze in the sun, enjoy forays into the local markets and generally eat and drink in a non-too healthy way. However, I always feel well and refreshed when I return. Although taking this time away from Sudeley when I really should be concentrating on getting ready for the forthcoming season usually creates a frantic and hectic rush to look forward to when I return.

This year, together with the Historic Royal Palaces and other Tudor houses throughout the country, we are planning to celebrate a very special event – the 500th anniversary of Henry VIII's accession to the throne. Sudeley belonged to the crown in the sixteenth century until it was given by Henry VIII's son, Edward VI, to Sir Thomas Seymour, who shortly after the King's death, married his sixth wife and widow, Queen Katherine Parr, and brought her to live at the castle.

In 2009 we are focusing on another important moment in the castle's Tudor history. In 1535 Henry VIII visited Sudeley with his then queen, Anne Boleyn, attended by a vast train of courtiers and baggage. While Henry and Anne Boleyn stayed in the castle many of their entourage were lodged at Winchcombe Abbey, where Thomas Cromwell, the Vicar General, was putting in hand the process that led to the Dissolution of the Monasteries.

Anne Boleyn meanwhile decided to investigate the relic of holy blood – said to have been Christ's blood – which was drawing many pilgrims to the nearby Abbey at Hailes. On examination it proved to be duck's blood which ran out by a system of hidden levers worked by the monks. When Anne told Henry of this trickery he ordered the false relic to be removed, but it seems the monks only did so for a time and it was soon replaced.

While writing this piece, my mind keeps wandering to the task of bringing to life this extraordinary moment in the history of Gloucestershire and Sudeley. Creating a new exhibition is a stimulating challenge involving much planning and research. February would be the ideal month to work on this, but what about Goa, sunshine and beaches? Decisions, decisions… almost as many as the excited brides-to-be who are planning their fairytale weddings.

A Victorian wedding at Sudeley.

Charles II Stumpwork box

The box would have been made by a girl in her early teens as a demonstration of her embroidery and needlework skills. It is covered with Biblical imagery and contains an astounding network of seven hidden compartments.

Spring

A Stitch In Time
March 2008

Emma Dent, Sudeley's nineteenth-century chatelaine, really was a most remarkable woman. I never cease to be impressed at the extent and thoroughness of her interests, activities and her vision in leaving behind such an eclectic and well-documented legacy of her life and times for future generations to rediscover.

About this time last year I was busy mounting an exhibition from the extensive, but as yet unacknowledged, collection of textiles housed here at Sudeley. Most of the items put on view had been stitched by or were personal items of Emma's, or they were acquired treasures for her small museum. It wasn't until they were assembled into the 'Long Room' that we really realised what riches had been revealed. Experts from the Royal School of Needlework and other knowledgeable bodies were consulted and proclaimed it to be a 'collection of national importance'! I, somewhat embarrassed and chagrined by my lack of knowledge and due respect shown to many of these pieces (i.e. some had been casually strewn about the house for decorative effect or packed away in unidentified boxes), soon became fascinated and truly amazed at the dedicated skills and patient commitment of past generations of women to this craft. Having made a few feeble attempts at cross-stitch myself, I can confidently vouch that fine needlework is not work for amateurs.

The run up after the winter months to reopening the castle to visitors is always frantic. In a rush last year and assisted by a few knowledgeable and generous volunteers, we put together a display of the body of the collection in record time and christened it 'Threads of Time'. This includes examples of textile techniques spanning 400 years from a magnificent seventeenth-century stumpwork casket, delicate lace, white work, costumes and furnishings to sumptuous silk wall hangings and woven tapestry. Emma Dent herself was a highly accomplished needlewoman and pieces of her own work including the altar cloth she embroidered for the Sudeley church are featured in the exhibition.

Its appeal and success with our visitors was instant and continuous. Surprisingly our gentlemen guests seemed equally fascinated with the collection and especially the modern work done by inmates of HM prisons for the charity Fine Cell work. My grandchildren are intrigued by the Charles II stumpwork casket with its seven tiny secret drawers and hiding places and we have now made a video showing how the casket can be taken apart and re-assembled.

The collection of samplers has been a great hit with school children who are amazed to learn that until recent times needlework was regarded as an essential part of a girl's education – starting from the age of six. Emma Dent ran a sewing class for the girls in Winchcombe when she found that they were 'lamentably ignorant of the needle'.

All this enthusiasm has encouraged us to remount, embellish and add to the collection as a permanent attraction at Sudeley. Last year we found that both children and adults were fascinated by the chance to try their hand at lace-making when members of local lace guilds and societies came to Sudeley to demonstrate their skills, and in 2008 we plan more demonstrations of embroidery and lace-making as well as workshops and lectures which will be built round a botanical theme, to complement our award-winning gardens.

Those who love textiles and needlework should not miss this

exhibition and I would encourage anyone, like myself, perhaps yet unacquainted with the astounding skills and variety of art forms of this medium, to come along and see the story which generations of tireless hands have woven for us.

Details of the Sheldon Tapestry. (See colour section.)

A letter from Charles Dickens

Emma Dent's Autograph Collection

'*I am beginning my autograph book and it promises well with the Duke of Wellington, Garibaldi and Paganini – by way of beginning*' *wrote Emma Dent in her diary on a Sunday evening in December 1863.*

Her final collection of distinguished autographs gathered with the help of friends and relatives includes: Literary lions: Sir Walter Scott, William Wordsworth, Lord Byron, Lord Tennyson, Henry Longfellow and William Makepeace Thackeray.

From the wider world of politics and medicine: Charles Darwin, David Livingstone, Edward Jenner (pioneer of vaccination), Cecil Rhodes, William Wilberforce, Lord Palmerston and Roland Hill (who started the penny post) as well as American Civil War letters from Andrew Jackson, Robert E. Lee and General Beauregard and a Civilian Pass issued by Abraham Lincoln.

All these are now on display in the Exhibition Room at Sudeley together with her correspondence with Florence Nightingale.

Sale Of The Century
April 2008

An increasingly popular weekend activity in my native land is the yard sale. Fanatics set their alarm clocks for ever-earlier starts in the competition to 'get there' ahead of the crowd and find the bargain of a lifetime. At a yard sale in Maine, where I was visiting my sister last year, there were two couples arguing over which of them had seen the green silk lampshade first, while I walked away with an amazingly useful computer bag at a satisfying knockdown price. What's this have to do with this month's 'Castle Connections', you may well ask? Well, translate yard sale – so-called as they are traditionally held in people's front gardens (less pleasingly called yards in US) – into car boot sale and you have the answer.

Sudeley is holding a castle car boot sale on 13 April, and I have started scouring and rummaging my way through years of hoarding and over-crowded cupboards to make the most of this useful opportunity. The problem is that I find it difficult to let go of things that hold memories of when, why and how they appeared in my life. Obviously past generations felt the same as the attics at Sudeley are begging for a little more breathing space, and I have decided to try and be ruthless.

Emma Dent, Sudeley's nineteenth-century chatelaine, was an avid and indefatigable collector and hoarder and I will never forget my amazement on my first visit to the Long Room, to find it piled high with dusty Victorian furniture and artefacts and stuffed with trunks and boxes bursting with the relics of her age which had been packed away during the first half of the twentieth century, because their style was no longer considered fashionable.

What fun it was to rediscover this era, and the contents of the trunks and dusty boxes in the Long Room soon became the source of our many exhibitions over the years depicting the life and times of Sudeley in its Victorian heyday. Thank you Emma for so carefully keeping, recording and cataloguing your life and possessions for us to see and enjoy today. It is fortunate that the boot sale wasn't a popular weekend activity in earlier years, as much of the furnishings and fashions we now appreciate at Sudeley today might have been recklessly abandoned to bargain seekers.

While writing this piece, I had an unannounced visit from my four-year-old grandson who had come to show me the latest find from his favourite sport, foraging for treasure around the garden. He said the shiny object in his muddy hand was an ancient coin, dropped by a knight while fighting off an invader. It looked more like a squashed bottle top to me but I am no expert on treasure trove, so didn't share my opinion. I was fascinated, however, to see how early our kind discovers the thrill of the hunt for hidden gold, and perhaps the yard/boot sales of today help to satisfy that eternal quest.

I apologise, to those who do not share this particular enthusiasm, for finishing this column with my favourite subject – my grandchildren. I have five. I used to dread the tedium of 'granny' conversations with friends who had joined this smug club before me. Now I can't wait to relate my latest cute anecdote in those circles, if I can ever get a word in edgeways.

A letter from Florence Nightingale.

Recipes from the Old Sudeley Recipe Book, *dating back to 1669.*

To make Sausages
Cut out all the flesh of a leg of mutton or veal. Shred it very small.
Add to it as much beef suet as meat. Shred very fine both together.
Then take near a pint of oysters well washed in their own liquor.
Beat them very well together in a mortar until they be well mixed
and the oysters not discerned. Season it with pepper and salt, mace
and nutmeg, but not too high: a little thyme savoury and safe, shred
very small. Mix this with 5 raw eggs, roll them in little rolls and fry
them in butter. These will be good if you have no oysters.

The Infallible Pudding
Take suet – one pound – shred very small, raisins of the sun – one
pound – stoned and cut, six eggs well beaten and 3 spoonfuls of fine
flour, two of sugar, half a nutmeg, some salt. Mix all together, tie it
close up in a cloth and boil it six hours.
Note: Your maid must rise early the day you make this pudding, or
you will dine late.

Mutton Stew And Marmalade
May 2008

I have just returned from a fascinating week in Florence with my art lecture group where we were immersed in the glories of that great Italian Renaissance city. I also took the opportunity to slip away and spend a few enjoyable days with my Italian brother-in-law and nephew in their charming rural home tucked away in the Umbrian Hills. He and my late and much missed sister-in-law Catherine created this small corner of paradise from a ruined farmstead of a couple of cowsheds and a pigsty (a task which looked barely imaginable when I first saw it over thirty-five years ago).

Echoes of Sudeley are scattered casually around the old stone rooms; family photographs, pictures, furniture and familiar objects from my mother-in-law's collection, which I came to know well over the years of her life here at Sudeley. Catherine was a connoisseur of fine things as well as a brilliant cook and many English friends and I have enjoyed unforgettably delicious and lazy days of hospitality with her and Franco over the years. Together they presided over a delightfully unconventional kitchen, cluttered with all the culinary necessities of great cooking, walls lined with racks of wine, music, books, dog baskets. Drink and conversation were always flowing, and a fiendish parrot usually screeching furiously in one corner. Ara the parrot is now around thirty-five years old and has lost most of his fine plumage, but still bad-tempered and in full voice, he occupies the same corner and anyone other than his master who ventures too close to his perch is unlikely to come away un-bloodied.

Franco has happily continued the tradition of great cooking for friends and family and I was treated to some memorable tastes and treats when there. However, one surprising relic of long ago life at Sudeley came with an unexpected surge of taste at breakfast from a large jar on his old oak table. It was the most delicious marmalade I have tasted since the days of old Mrs Bell, who was my mother-in-law's cook at Sudeley over forty years ago. Mrs Bell, a cosy and kindly woman, was not particularly renowned or appreciated for her post war philosophy of cooking, which tended towards the overcooked and under flavoured school, with the exception of her puddings, cakes and marmalade. I remember well the sinking expressions of family and guests as we pushed the mutton stew or boiled tongue around our plates, until rescue came in the form of a heavenly crisp apple charlotte, munchy blackberry crumble, mouth-watering bread and butter pudding, or my favourite, sticky toffee pudding, and all accompanied by my mother-in-law's prize-winning thick double cream from the Home Farm.

Catherine obviously didn't inherit her mother's disinterest in food, but cleverly carried away with her Mrs Bell's best recipes, amongst which was the famous marmalade now precisely and caringly reproduced by Franco, along with her ginger cake and lime/mint jelly, to the accompaniment of Ara's raunchy conversation. I am including the marmalade recipe here for those who wish to give it a go and was told that the real secret is in the quick boiling at the end.

Another delight of the Italian table is that there is no nonsense about fat free, wheat free, calorie counting, watching carbs or any of the spoil-sport guilt making propaganda we are subjected to… and no one appeared any the worse for wear from it. I did notice, however, that my jeans seemed a little snug when I struggled into them this morning.

Orange Marmalade (Mrs Bell's)

6 Seville oranges (about 2lbs.)
2 sweet oranges
1 Lemon
6 pints water
6lbs. sugar

Wash fruit, cut in half, squeeze out the juice and pips and slice the peel finely.
Put the sliced fruit in a bowl add the juice and the pips tied in a muslin bag, cover with water and leave overnight if possible.
Next day put the fruit in a preserving pan and cook gently for 2 hours or until the peel is quite soft.
Remove the bag of pips, add the sugar, stir until this is dissolved then boil quickly until setting point is reached.
Yield 10lbs.

African Solutions to African Problems (ASAP) supports community-based organisations of women caring for orphans and vulnerable children affected by HIV/AIDS.

We are currently working with six pioneer community-based organisations made of up 585 women supporting 8,500 orphans and vulnerable children in more than 112 community drop-in and daycare centres in impoverished communities in South Africa.

A key aspect of ASAP support is to provide capacity-building interventions that help the groups to develop their organisations, improve their services and attain their own development goals.

ASAP has demonstrated that grassroots organisations and their social networks of women are capable of scaling up and replicating effective models of care for orphans and vulnerable children.

Based on practical experience, ASAP has developed a unique seven-year model of community-based intervention that builds the capacity of emerging groups to develop into mature organisations with a community network to care for the majority of orphans and vulnerable in their community.

ASAP is expanding our model to a further six community-based organisations. By allowing them to develop their own models of care, in conjunction with training, gardens and regular onsite capacity building visits, these organisations and their networks of women will reach an additional 12,000 orphans and vulnerable children.

A Grandmother's Call To Arms
March 2009

As the proud Grandmother of five it is difficult not to refer to some recent anecdote that involves one or more of them. Becoming a Grandmother, especially for the first time, is a miraculous and awe-inspiring event. Grandchildren are different from one's own children as they can be loved and enjoyed more objectively and at the same time deliver the delight, warmth and the unique joys of discovery which babies and young children bring into a family. The role of Grannies (and Grandpas) in family life is privileged and vital because we can, and sometimes must, do things for our grandchildren that parents cannot do.

Elders hold knowledge and wisdom to share with younger generations. I'm not sure I would qualify in this category as I have been accused of being soft on some of the rules: the forbidden fruits of chocolate biscuits before bedtime (proven to cause a sugar rush and burst of energy) another story or game after official lights out (bad moods next morning) pillow fights, bed jumping, water fights and the like – none of which are conducive to an easy transition into dreamland. In the spirit of not disturbing tired and busy mummy and daddy with unimportant details, these small deceptions can create a friendly conspiratorial bond between the parties concerned.

My friend and renowned gardening authority, Jane Fearnley-Whittingstall, who designed the Queen's Garden with me at Sudeley, has embraced grannyhood in a major way. Her popular published books, *The Good Granny Guide* and *Good Granny Cookbook* are an invaluable help with ideas to creatively amuse, entertain and feed the little treasures in ways that their parents would approve. It also advises how **not** to interfere and to hold one's tongue when longing to speak out with what might be unwelcome wisdom to daughter or daughter-in-law.

Jane has very generously offered a donation from the sale of her latest publication *The Good Granny Companion* to a charity campaign close to my heart, Grannies United for ASAP. We are both founder members of a group of grandmothers in this country who have united to raise awareness and funds for the 'Gogos' – severely impoverished Grandmothers in South Africa who have courageously taken responsibility for their AIDS orphans and vulnerable grandchildren. This initiative was started by another remarkable friend, Pricilla Higham, who seven years ago formed African Solution to African Problems, of which Grandmothers United is a part. We raise funds which go directly to the 'Gogos' within the ASAP communities.

Recently, I was touched when many African grandmothers and their orphaned children stayed at Sudeley on a fundraising mission. The children at first shyly but soon enthusiastically joined in games with my grandchildren and friends. One delightful boy, ten-year-old Saipo, was an adept magician as well as acrobat and could do a running flip without touching the ground. My grandson Lucien was so impressed that a gleam of pure hero worship shone in his eye when asking for repeat performances. Poor Saipo was exhausted by the demands, but a lasting friendship was forged and we correspond regularly.

It is worth looking at www.africansolutions.org to see the amazing success and progress of this charity now supporting 12,000 children and over 1,000 carers. Grandmothers United for ASAP (GU) is inviting grandmothers from all parts of the UK to join us in giving small tea parties or other gatherings to raise funds to support our struggling sister grandmothers in SA.

Our policy is no minimum or maximum donation and the tea parties are a great way to see one's friends, enjoy sharing stories about our own grandchildren and to give back something of our good fortune. I hope some of my readers might join us in hosting a 'tea party'. For more details please contact Camilla Corbett, Camilla@africansolutions.org, who will supply you with all the information and a CD to show the work of ASAP to your guests.

While writing this I became aware of a commotion coming from just outside my sitting room window. Upon investigation I found two of my grandchildren, who live in another part of the castle, in an accelerating altercation over whose turn it was to throw the ball for the dog. However, this opportunity to restore peace and forgiveness with a few kindly grandma's words got me embroiled in many angry accusations between the two disagreeing parties. Wisdom and experience to the rescue, and with a swift suggestion of a chocolate biscuit, calm again reigned. Uh oh, the lunch gong sounded from their quarters and so – with a quick wipe of telltale smudges around the gills and a wink – I hurried my charges off in that direction.

The Duke of Bedford opening the Royal Sudeley exhibition, 1970.

Acting Out A Scene From History
April 2009

I left off in February deliberating on whether to join my friends on what has become an annual holiday house party in Goa, or to buckle down to the business in hand at Sudeley – mounting this year's exhibition to celebrate the 500th anniversary of Henry VIII's accession to the throne.

Well, not surprisingly, I chose the Goan option, and while the rest of Gloucestershire was slipping and sliding and digging itself out of snowdrifts, I was basking in glorious sunshine with my book in hand, often accompanied by an exotic cocktail, and giving barely a fleeting thought to Henry VIII and his struggles with queens, priests and issues of monarchy.

How quickly the landscape can change, however, and today, under grey skies and groggy with jetlag, I donned my overalls and immersed myself in acrylic paint and bunting as assistant to our talented 'in house' artist Katie Morgan. Katie is a local freelance artist but over the years she has helped in the creation and mounting of so many exhibitions at Sudeley that we like to think of her as our own resident artist. She has the amazing ability to interpret a vague wave of hand and idea of mine into a thoroughly exciting and professional result.

This year's production will not disappoint. We have a great and little known intrigue to illustrate which involves two of history's most celebrated characters, Henry VIII and Anne Boleyn. I will say no more lest I spoil the surprise but events took place in Winchcombe in 1535 that changed the course of English history forever.

Creating exhibitions around some of the extraordinary events and people that the castle has hosted over its long history has been a fascinating and enjoyable part of my life and work here. As a self-proclaimed production manager, I have had the most incredible material to work with. Who couldn't tell a good tale with the likes of Richard III, Henry VIII and his six wives, Elizabeth I, King Charles I and Oliver Cromwell (to name but a few) walking on and off stage at various decades in the Sudeley story? Emma Dent, the Victorian chatelaine, was fortunately so fascinated by the castle's past owners, their lives and customs that she did much of the groundwork in researching and collecting the historical and personal items which we use to illustrate the 'drama' that is on view here today.

Having been dragged around dry and musty old museums in my youth and endured the whingeing of my own children when a visit to a 'stately' was suggested, I have tried to present Sudeley's art treasures and history in a different and entertaining way. I was introduced to this theatrical concept of presentation when Mark and I first decided to open the castle to the public in 1970. It didn't seem very interesting as it stood and we consulted the well-known theatre and opera designer and friend Adam Pollock for ideas. Little did we realise where Adam's imagination and talent would take us. The result was *Royal Sudeley*, a unique and exciting indoor interactive adventure through the history of Sudeley – meeting it's protagonists head on, whether in the privacy of Katherine Parr's bedroom, walking the steps to the scaffold with Thomas Seymour, mourning with Lady Jane Grey at Katherine's funeral or dancing at the three day celebration given for Queen Elizabeth's visit in the autumn of 1592. *Royal Sudeley* was proclaimed throughout the land as a most original presentation of historical material, and Sudeley's reputation was on its way. The show went on for several years but eventually the gargantuan computer that ran it (taking up a whole room) became obsolete and it was necessary to move on to new attractions. At any rate, I learned my trade under a master, which has given me inspiration for the many exhibitions that followed *Royal Sudeley* and brought us up to this year's celebration.

Well, all talk and no action… I had better roll my sleeves up and get back to work if we are to open on time.

Mark and Elizabeth in the Banqueting Hall ruins.

I Am Not Moving Into A Cowshed!
May 2009

The month of May is soon upon us when flowers and trees start to blossom in the warmer weather. It is said to be a time of love and romance when people celebrate the coming of summer with many different customs that are expressions of joy and hope after a long winter. This year particularly, with the hard reality of the economic crisis, the enormity of global problems and the uncertainty of the future, we all need something to celebrate and to take our minds temporarily off worldly cares.

Across Britain, this is likely to be a year in which fewer recession-struck families take holidays abroad and will thus be testing the charms of a British holiday. Recent statistics show that numbers of visitors to National Trust properties have already risen fifty per cent on last year. This is music to the ears of owners of privately owned historic houses like Sudeley, who do not have the powerful marketing resources of National Trust properties behind them, but will nevertheless hope to benefit from the current economic mood of staying at home – avoiding the nightmare experiences of frantic airports, cancelled flights, disappointing promises of 'luxury' overpriced holidays on overcrowded and polluted beaches, and instead will venture out to discover the glories and beauty of yet unspoiled rural England and our own unique history and heritage.

Sudeley is lucky in being able to tick most of the boxes of 'a perfect British day out destination'. It sits majestically in one of the top beauty spots of England where the ancient Cotswold hills begin to slope gently down to the Evesham valley and beyond to the sea.

The castle's history is unsurpassed, great and celebrated personalities have lived here and its prize-winning gardens have been listed among the top ten gardens in the country.

Well, what more can one ask for? I have lived in this magical, often demanding, place for over forty years and if I can string it out until 2012, I will have lived at Sudeley for fifty years and survived a longer occupation and kinder fate than many of its past residents – Richard III, Ralph Boteler, Thomas Seymour, Lady Jane Grey, and Lord Chandos all met a murky end in one way or another. I marvel at the stamina of the nobility of past generations at a time when Machiavellian schemes and bloody plans to unseat them were lurking behind every door.

So far the security of my tenure has been more peaceful, that is until a recent bit of journalistic chicanery reported in the local press that our family was soon to move into a cowshed, due to the financial squeeze. I suspect a clever but mischievous journalist with a sense of humour saw the notice of my daughter's application for planning permission to convert a beautiful but derelict seventeenth-century barn into a residence to give it new life and purpose.

This snippet was soon taken up by the national and international media, probably as an attempt to lighten up the constant diet of gloomy recession news. My sister, who lives in Long Island, New York, saw it on the internet and had a good laugh picturing me with a bandanna around my head and shouldering bundles of corn for the cows. My son in Hawaii thought it was hilarious and the story, I would guess, has brought a smile to the face of many others. Meanwhile, I have been fending off the comments and commiserations of friends and neighbours on the family's bad fortune.

The American humourist Mark Twain said in a curt cable to

the *Associated Press* following an account of his recent demise while travelling in Europe (*c.* 1900) 'The report of my death was an exaggeration'!

Taking liberties from Twain I say, 'The report of my move to a cowshed was an exaggeration', or at any rate premature until I have done my best to break the record of living at Sudeley longer than any of its previous owners. My family and I remain very much in residence and are looking forward to welcoming hoards of visitors this summer to celebrate all that is good in the British holiday at home.

The falconer, Gary Cope.

Is Sudeley For The Birds?

My two husbands, Mark and Harry, had much in common. They were great friends, both married to me (though not at the same time!) and had a passion for birds... of the feathered variety I should emphasise!

The ancient sport of falconry has become a popular attraction for stately homes and leisure parks throughout the kingdom as well as a sport practiced by many professional and amateur enthusiasts.

With a certain smugness I claim that Sudeley was the first house to show and put on falconry displays, soon followed hot on our heels by other owners and tourist attractions. 'Imitation is the best form of flattery,' but in this case larger centres with more falconers and birds of prey attracted thousands of visitors while our resident falconer Gary and his sponsor, my enthusiastic husband Harry, were more interested in developing an exclusive unique breeding program of rare birds in captivity. Our falconry displays for visitors to the castles were discontinued in favour of the breeding program, but the area where they took place is still referred to as the Falcon Lawn.

The Old Bothy, originally intended for housing farm labourers, soon became luxury accommodation to such exotic species as the Peregrine, Gyr and Saker falcon as well as the more common Hawk. Successful breeding was a complicated procedure starting first with the male bird bonding (falling in love) with his keeper. This was followed by all sorts of enticements and delicacies such as day old chicks and mating clucking and gurgling noises simulated by the beloved master. With any luck the intended father to be would cooperate and further complicated procedures would hurriedly take place – not unlike our modern fertility clinics. A successful impregnation coming to full term was a rare but thrilling event and incubators and twenty-four hours feeding schedules would keep the falconer and his assistant on round the clock duty until the baby bird could fend for itself.

My favourite expedition to the Bothy was to see the Snowy Owls, also kept for breeding purposes, but more often visited by my children and our guests to coo over for their enchanting and adorable white faces with bright yellow eyes. Gary would let us gently stroke the baby owls and their feathers were so soft that with eyes closed you would hardly know that your fingers had met with another surface.

Because of the steely looks of our estate manager when doing his book balancing, and more particularly the failure of the rare Gyr Falcon to produce enough progeny to keep the business 'flying', our beautiful birds were found new homes and a very special chapter of life at Sudeley was over. But who knows, the Snowy Owls and eagled-eyed hawks of prey may return again in the future in the same way as our beautiful pheasants have now come back to roost.

Mark was devoted to his collection of rare pheasants. In the late 1960s he mounted an expedition to Nepal with Major Ian Graham to bring back the first Blood Pheasant to England and to add to his menagerie. Displayed in a colourful maze of pens in the garden, the pheasantry became a popular attraction for visitors and soon extended to include other exotic birds and animals including monkeys, a coati mundi, ostriches and the like.

I remember one Christmas a wallaby feeling poorly was

brought into the house for closer observation and a bemused on duty vet was called away from his Christmas pudding to be in attendance. Some rare birds and animals required diets of specialities which could only be imported from costly faraway places. After Mark died, trying to keep his collection housed, fed and suitably mated became an overhead which caused our then practically minded accountant to cough and splutter. The pheasantry sadly closed its pens a few years later, but now, thirty years on, the rare breeds have been re-collected by Sudeley's estate foreman John Sherlock, relocated in a dramatic setting behind the Moat Pond and are now happily pecking, living and nesting without complaint in their adopted English environment. It is a joy to have them back.

The Queen's Garden.

The Gardens

Sudeley's gardens are cradled in a fold of the Cotswolds, sheltered by hills in most directions but somewhat exposed to the fierce prevailing winds from the south-west. There are fine pastoral views and although there can be hard frosts in winter the alkaline soil is reasonably fertile. The gardens are framed by romantic stone buildings, magnificent trees, sweeping lawns and wide stretches of still water. However, they cannot be entirely appreciated or understood without some knowledge of the castle's history or the more recent circumstances which led to our current programme of planting and restoration.

My late mother-in-law, Mary Dent-Brocklehurst, was the guiding influence in the gardens from the 1930s until she handed over the castle to her son Mark, my husband, and myself in 1969. He inherited his mother's love of gardening but until then had only practised this burgeoning interest in creating our delightful small garden in London. Taking charge of the Sudeley gardens was something he greatly looked forward to and I, frankly somewhat of a philistine in this area, supported the plan with enthusiasm. Sadly, however, it wasn't to be as he died suddenly in 1972 soon after we had taken up residence in the castle.

I had no thoughts about the gardens at that time and concentrated instead on trying to make the castle into a home for our children and a visitor attraction, as we had planned. My lack of interest naturally proved to be short-sighted and as the passing years took their toll, Mary's lovely borders and roses became sad and neglected, and the gardens rather an embarrassment to the castle's growing reputation as a place to visit.

Fortunately, when I realised the necessity to address this I wasn't foolhardy enough to think that looking through coffee table books and pointing to pretty pictures could solve the problem. Instead I consulted the distinguished garden designer and friend, the late Lanning Roper. On seeing the task ahead I think he immediately felt a little weary, but helpfully suggested some simplifications and replacement of plants in the formal garden. He also introduced me to Rosemary Verey who a few years later I commissioned to design and oversee a new planting in the Secret Garden to house the delightful eighteenth-century lead putti (since stolen), which I had found in Ireland. The new garden was to celebrate my remarriage to Lord Ashcombe in 1979. The thrill of watching it blossom into life must have triggered the realisation that it was time for me to try and undertake the renewal of all of Sudeley's surroundings, and from some unknown and untested realm of my imagination ideas began to form. It was with the garden designer Jane Fearnley-Whittingstall that a more structured interpretation of our collated thoughts began to take shape. She was most patient with me, as I must have had some fairly wacky ideas, but with the combination of the blind leading the guide the castle's surroundings magically started to realise a new energy of growth and individuality.

No rules have shaped Sudeley's gardens of today; the only framework being its long history and past owners, the timeless tranquillity of the picturesque buildings and romantic ruins, and the magnificent yew hedges planted by Emma Dent in the nineteenth century. The setting is a natural stage on which to recreate the legacy of the castle's history, handed down the ages from one generation to another. The satisfaction of creating new gardens has become my greatest pleasure and seems to inspire even more ideas, which wouldn't be possible without the tolerance, dedication and expertise of various garden design 'guru's and our small hard working garden team. Latterly I have been working with Charles Chesshire, an expert and writer on clematis, who has introduced hundreds of new plants in many varieties throughout the garden. It is this challenge and rewarding partnership of talents that has ignited my interest and perhaps even passion for the garden, which no one, least of all myself, would have expected when I arrived at Sudeley, the quintessential 'townie', all those years ago.

The appeal of Sudeley and its surroundings has for generations attracted the artist's eye, and painters and photographers from near and far visit the castle today to capture some of its haunting beauty. I feel incredibly lucky, as living here has enabled me to witness some of those mystical moments when nature's secrets are revealed in all the subtleties of light, colour, form and scent. I hope that everyone who visits may too experience something of the garden's magic.

Royal Roses

Among the 100 varieties of roses represented at Sudeley are the red rose of Lancaster, the personal standard of Queen Eleanor of Aquitaine, and the white rose of York; the two roses which, united, became the emblem of the Tudors Sudeley's royal owners in the sixteenth century. Here too, is the striped gallica Rosa mundi, named after the victim of Queen Eleanor's jealousy. Fair Rosamund, the mistress of King Henry II, died young, so the rumours went on the orders of the queen. This rose was said to be Anne Boleyn's favourite and was planted in the Tudor parterre where later Katherine Parr and her young protégé, Lady Jane Grey, strolled amongst the fragrant herbs and flowers on soft summer evenings.

Summer

Smelling Like Roses
June 2008

The Sudeley Castle Gardens will soon explode in a firework display of old roses with their subtle variety of colours, textures and fragrances and will again weave their enchantment for all to enjoy and marvel at. I love roses and I love this time of year in the garden.

The history of the rose stretches back to the dawn of civilisation and man's fascination with this glorious species has continued to the present day. I am not alone in choosing the rose as my favourite flower. However, when asked which is my favourite rose, I'm at a loss amongst the abundance of choice, except that I feel honour-bound to mention the Tudor Rose, which has become Sudeley's emblem.

Twenty years ago I embarked with Jane Fearnley-Whittingstall, a renowned authority on roses on an ambitious project to recreate a rose garden on the original Tudor parterre that had been laid for Queen Katherine Parr when she came to live at Sudeley after marrying Sir Thomas Seymour. The hundreds of roses which we then selected for what is now called the Queen's Garden, reflect every period of the castle's history, from the time when Katherine and Lady Jane Grey strolled the petal-strewn paths until the present day.

Roses evoke different reactions in different people depending on which particular aspect captures their imagination. The universal attraction of the species and its history is a subject too great to tackle in this short article, but for me its greatest charm is the variety of scents, from the most subtle to the most complex and sumptuously perfumed. Fragrance, it has been said, is the 'soul' of the rose and is too elusive to pin down, as it has no tangible substance. It seems to exist in some other dimension.

While musing on this ethereal idea, I was rudely brought back from my reverie by my dog Kola, who burst into the room, full of enthusiasm and the joys of spring. It didn't take long to realise why she was so pleased with herself. Her favourite country pursuit, handed down from primitive ancestors, was painfully obvious. She had been having a good roll in some foul and undesirable substance and wanted to share the pleasure of this exotic perfume with her mistress. It must have been disappointing when without praise or congratulation she was sharply invited to leave the house and sent to be hosed down in cold water. With this interruption, my theme of scent was challengingly brought into focus but continuing along the original lines I began some research on the secret of the roses' hidden knowledge of fragrance. There appears to be no answer to this intriguing question.

Nature is a skilled perfumier, having worked its art through hundreds of years of cross breeding. The repertoire of scents it creates is unending; from the unique spicy aroma of a myrrh-scented rose such as St Cecilia to the luxurious sweet smelling Gertrude Jekyll, or the fresh fragrance of English Roses to the sharp fruity smell of a Rambler Rose like Rambling Rector.

Scents have great power to move us emotionally, working on deep associations in our memory, but it is hard to find appropriate words to describe the subtle variations in smell that the nose recognises. Animals have a highly evolved sense of smell, thousands of times more powerful than our own, but even so, we too can get the most sublime pleasure from the sweet smell of a rose.

Kola is now back, looking and smelling more presentable, and all is forgiven. I see that she was just indulging in the seductive attraction of scent, very much the same as my ramblings in the last few paragraphs.

I hope readers who are as fascinated by roses as I am will visit the Sudeley Gardens in the summer. I don't think you will be disappointed.

Emma Dent.

*Emma's stored treasures, diaries and memories of her life and times
are displayed at Sudeley – These were her bones, but I like to think
that her spirit lives on in the great avenue of beech trees which she
planted on the main drive to the Castle, so that they would 'grow up
and cast their pretty shadows and spread their arms to catch the rays
of the sun – and men and women would walk by them and children
play under them, even when there was no-one left to remember the
old lady who lovingly planted them'.*

Extract from The Lady of Sudeley *by Jean Bray.*

The Lady Of Sudeley
July 2009

Anyone who comes to Sudeley Castle soon becomes aware of Emma Dent. Her hand is evident everywhere – in the castle buildings, in its treasured and historical contents and in the gardens, which she loved and planned so well. However, it seemed to me that everyone knew what Emma had done but that very little was known about her as a person.

This was so until some years ago when I began to explore a pile of trunks and packing cases, which had remained tucked away in the castle's old Long Room, untouched for nearly a century. There I discovered the stored treasures of Emma's life, an amazing collection of diaries, scrapbooks, letters, clothes and lace, all of which we have since used to create at Sudeley a permanent exhibition of her life and times. Her diaries have formed the basis of a book *The Lady of Sudeley* written by writer and journalist Jean Bray, who is also our archivist. This picture of life in a Victorian country house shows Emma to be a vigorous and lively woman with a clear and modern mind for her times, a lady with a ready wit and a strong will.

Over the years I have admired, been inspired, moved and even sometimes intimidated by getting to know Emma through her diaries and possessions. Without the benefit of yoga classes, exercise machines, calorie counters, and endless healthy advice from gurus and women's magazines, her constitution and mental energy were astounding, even into old age; this was mainly achieved by walking, reading good books and having pure thoughts – well, most of the time, anyway! Occasional perverse entries creep into her diaries, usually provoked by one of her pet antagonists (the neighbouring aristocrat, the vicar, her husband's gout, her ungrateful relations, views and politics not akin to her own and other niggling annoyances which we can all at times relate to).

Winchcombe town and its surrounds, estate employees, pensioners and animal welfare were amongst the beneficiaries of her enormous kindness and generosity, setting a precedent that only the wealthiest and saintliest of future owners of Sudeley could measure up to.

Her personal furniture, curtains, bedspreads, pictures and other household items, which are not on display, are still sprinkled around our rooms to call our own. I must even admit to once or twice taking the liberty of 'borrowing' from her wardrobe. Mixing modern with vintage is now very much in fashion and, waiting for the right moment, I have had my eye on her exquisite embroidered velvet coat by Worth of Paris *c.* 1850, which is on display in the museum. Regrettably, however, I think that moment has passed. At my son's recent birthday celebration we started off with a reception in the old Long Room, now our exhibition centre. As his guests meandered through Sudeley's treasures with flutes of champagne in hand, it wasn't long before a particularly svelte beauty asked to try on the coat. Carefully disengaged from the dummy and lifted on to the slim frame of the gorgeous guest, it was a perfect fit. Accompanied by exclamations of admiration and approval, it was then that I conceded that I might not be the right model to do justice to the precious piece, even if I did have the right occasion. After all, these heirlooms are for posterity, not to be flounced around in by would-be fashionista grannies, better advised to stick to their tweed skirts and a pinch of old lace.

It is fun to write light-heartedly about Emma, her life and

times, as well as the other fascinating past owners of the castle. However, their lives were also poignant, outstanding and sometimes lonely and tragic. I am not a historian and can't do justice to the deeper meanings the study of the past brings to the understanding of ourselves and where we come from. However, whenever I dip again into the pages of *The Lady of Sudeley*, I discover another layer of the mores, ideas and the social customs of this community in the Victorian era, unveiled through Emma's personal thoughts and observations. It is an absorbing insight into one woman's daily life, which she may or may not have intended sharing with us 150 years later.

Charles I bed.

Guiding Lights
July 2008

Sudeley, as might be expected, becomes a hive of activity in the summer months. Visitors in their numbers arrive from near and far, children on holiday rush to the adventure playground, an exciting schedule of events starts to unfold on an almost daily basis, and my family seem to invite everyone they know to drop in, often unexpectedly, for play, refreshment and general good times. It is a happy time of year – weather permitting. Last year as we all remember weather did not permit and many of our plans were washed away in the rains and floods. However, we are keeping all things crossed for a long and brilliant 2008 season.

People for the most part enjoy visiting Sudeley and over the years I have received many kind letters attesting to this. I recently opened a letter from a lady from Guernsey and am still purring with pleasure at her glowing comments about the garden and tour of the private wing where she said her party was joined by my six-year-old grandson who filled in some missing facts, unknown even to our learned guide, about life and items of interest in the castle – with special attention to his train set.

It is not always plain sailing for our in-house experts and I am reminded of a challenging moment a few years back as told by one of our senior guides, now retired, Alan Brandt. People often good-naturedly enjoy catching the guides out, and in this instance Alan was showing around a particularly inquisitive and probing group. Amongst them was a somewhat rattled father with a truculent and restless five-year-old boy. Addressing the child, Alan asked him what he was interested in and was informed that he had come to see where the dragon lived. A wink from the father who mouthed 'try and talk yourself out of that one' activated Alan's creative resources and he quickly replied that it was a pity that they had not telephoned before their long journey because there was a whole family of dragons who lived at the castle including a baby named 'Cedric' but they had all gone to the seaside for their holiday, all except Cedric, who was too young for the long trip. He was very shy and asleep under a big pile of grass in the car park where they would be able to see his hot breath streaming out of the top. Luckily Alan had noticed the gardeners' slow burning rubbish fire when he arrived that morning, and soon after he received a message from the father saying, 'well done'!

We've entertained some pranksters too. Once, many years ago, Iris, the head guide who was responsible for the security and efficient running of the rooms on view, was called on the security phone to come urgently to the Chandos Bedroom. A group of young revellers were bouncing on the Charles I bed, one wearing a bowler hat and all in a high state of inebriation and abandon. More accustomed to helping older people navigate the staircase or find their umbrellas, Iris and our other shocked guides, inexperienced in such behaviour and 'language', were called on to act as bouncers, and that tale has gone down in the annals of Sudeley ever since.

I could write a book called Good Guide Stories and may continue this theme another time. There never seems a dull or even repetitive day at Sudeley... well occasionally during the long grey winter months but we won't dwell on that now.

Lest 'summers lease hath all to short a date' I am rejoicing in the coming of the longest day, the thoughts of balmy evenings under the stars, the energetic enthusiasm of children, picnics, flowers, summer scents, and all the other sublime gifts of this time of year, should we be so lucky. May the heavens think kindly on us this summer… we deserve a good one.

Elizabeth preparing for a costume exhibition.

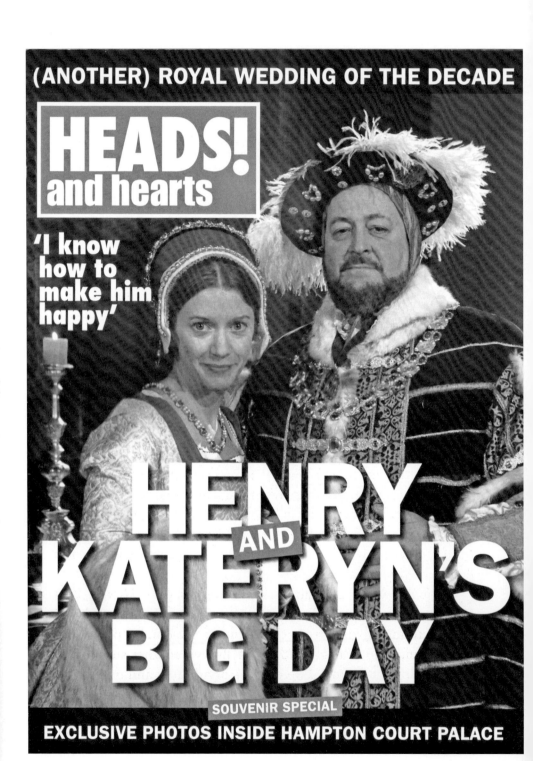

(ANOTHER) ROYAL WEDDING OF THE DECADE

HEADS!
and hearts

'I know how to make him happy'

HENRY AND KATERYN'S BIG DAY

SOUVENIR SPECIAL

EXCLUSIVE PHOTOS INSIDE HAMPTON COURT PALACE

Romance Among The Roses
August 2008

I have just counted up and realise that this is the twelfth 'Castle Connections' piece I have written for *Cotswold Life,* having submitted the first for last September's issue. 'Well, how is it going' I ask myself? Over the past months I have received several encouraging comments, and recently when I attended a science lecture in Cheltenham THREE people came up to me to say they were enjoying the column. Now three isn't exactly a standing ovation and certainly not enough to develop a swollen head about, but it is very nice and helpful to have feedback, whether positive or negative. My hope is that readers will find something interesting in the current every day activities of the castle, interwoven with its fascinating and sometimes haunting historic past. There is also our family life at the castle, which is unique only to the extent that we carry it out in the midst of the above, which occasionally throws up some curious and challenging situations.

I have been enjoying the current ITV3 *Henry VIII* series and last night's episode recreated Henry's cruel and cataclysmic divorce from Catherine of Aragon, his passionate and tumultuous affair with Anne Boleyn and her subsequent beheading on trumped up charges of adultery and incest, and all because of Henry's desperate need for a legitimate male heir to secure the Tudor dynasty's succession to the throne. Sadly, neither of those unlucky ladies was able to deliver an offspring of the desired gender to satisfy the king's desire. Ironically, Elizabeth, his daughter with Anne, became the greatest Tudor sovereign of them all.

Although Sudeley's Tudor associations are strongest with Queen Katherine Parr, Henry VIII, who then owned the castle, visited it in July 1535 with Queen Anne Boleyn. Legend has it that they strolled romantically through the rose garden and planted the fragrant *Rosa Mundi* rose to commemorate their visit.

Earlier today I went to the rose garden, now recreated on the original Tudor parterre, and was having a few enjoyable private moments imagining Henry and Anne, looking very much like Ray Winstone and Helena Bonham-Carter from the night before, tumbling from the yew hedges, laughing, holding hands, he plucking a scented rose to hand to her etc. etc., when a lady visitor jolted me back from my reverie to ask if I was the owner of the castle. 'I'd love to ask you a question,' she enthused, and I, hoping that it wasn't the name of some unusual plant or other tricky fact that should be known by the owner, tried to look alert. 'It must be wonderful living in a place where such exciting and romantic things happen' or words to that effect. She waxed on excitedly, and I thought 'how extraordinary, I was just thinking the same thing myself!' I was about to open up a discussion with some keenness on lovers such as Henry and Anne, or Katherine Parr and Thomas Seymour, or walking in the same steps as history's great and good and so on, when she beat me to the point by asking what was Liz Hurley's wedding like, had I met her and what about her dress? Well, umm, somewhat deflated and brought down to earth, what could I say but that it was all marvellous and that the bride was beautiful and make a hasty excuse to retreat from the scene.

What will fascinate people 500 years from now? Will the old stones of Sudeley still be standing and might they host some intergalactic celebrity of their day?

John Coucher Dent and Emma Dent as Henry VIII and Katherine Parr in costume for their Historical Party in 1859.

The War Years – 1940-1945

Sudeley became a 'safe house' for a third of the Tate Gallery's painting collection during the Second World War. Sir John Rothenstein, the Director sent this thank you letter.

I must also now say how extremely grateful I and my Trustees are for the shelter which you have given the Tate pictures during the war years. I must also thank you and your wife on my own, and on Ironside's behalf, and on that of all the members of the staff for your kindness in enabling so many of us to live in your house for such a protracted period. I shall certainly look back on my stay at Sudeley as a most agreeable way of spending a part of the war.
Once more please accept all my thanks for your hospitality.

The Tailor And The Housemaid
November 2007

I never cease to be in awe at how beautiful the gardens are in the evening of a fine summer's day, with the castle and rolling green hills as a backdrop. How lucky I am, who, after the visitors have left, can witness the exquisite play of light on the mullion windows sparkling like the facets on a rose cut diamond set in the soft golden hues of ancient Cotswold stone. I selfishly love this time to myself but will occasionally share it with another, provided I think they are in the right frame of mind to appreciate such a magical meander pre 'the cocktail hour'.

'The splendour falls on castle walls. And snowy summits old in glory'. But before I get carried away with purple prose, which I may return to later, I want to tell you of some others who have been equally transported by these ethereal moments of enchantment.

Sudeley Castle and its setting have often been described by writers as romantic, and even as the most romantic castle in England. It is true that some very high profile love affairs have taken place within its environs, including that of Henry VIII and Anne Boleyn, who strolled together in the gardens here in 1535, and Katherine Parr, who, soon after the death of the elderly king, married her first true love Thomas Seymour and passed her remaining short but happiest days under his roof at Sudeley.

Also there was a rumoured flirtation between Thomas and

Princess Elizabeth, who was then Katherine's young companion and protégé, but Elizabeth was too clever to take the roguish Thomas's advances too seriously and later, when she heard that he had been executed, said, 'This day dies a man with much wit and very little judgement'.

All this cavorting and carrying on at the castle, however, is not only confined to the past as often romance continues here today with many young couples choosing Sudeley for their marriages and wedding celebrations. I was married in the small fifteenth-century church in the garden, as were both my children, Henry and Mollie, and I can't think of a lovelier or more perfect setting for these occasions.

My favourite love story, however, started at Sudeley during the last war when what is now the visitor's car park became the prisoner of war camp for Italian and German prisoners who worked on the surrounding farmlands. The Brocklehurst family were on friendly terms with several of the prisoners and the children often went down to the fenced and barbed wire area and chatted with them.

One Italian inmate was a fine tailor and as soon as his skills were noted he was invited up to the castle to make clothes for the family. Mark remembered him as a jolly fellow, but was none too delighted with the suit and long trousers he made for him out of an old green woollen curtain. Clothes rationing at the time and his parents' practical philosophy didn't stretch to investing in a new tweed for an adolescent's first suit.

During the hours stitching in the castle the tailor became acquainted with a pretty young housemaid, and managed, even under the eagle eye of the fearsome housekeeper Janet, to court and woo her. After the war he sent for her and they were happily married for fifty years until she died.

My mother-in-law had told me this touching story and when a few years ago I was summoned by one of our guides to the North Hall as a visitor had requested to see me, I immediately knew him to be the tailor, now an elderly widower, who had returned to the scene of his courtship and where this great love had blossomed.

On meeting our eyes filled with tears and, in order to pull ourselves together, he joined me for a cup of tea. He told me about the children visiting the prisoners of war and that the family had been very kind to him. He continued to correspond with my mother-in-law over the years and I believe she paid for the young housemaid's trousseau and her journey to Italy.

The above examples of romance at Sudeley revolve around human love and attraction. But I see the romance of Sudeley in another form as well. It is a place where a sense of wonder and mystery can pervade everyday reality, where the senses are seduced and the imagination is tantalised into other worldly expression, and where artists through the ages, photographers and now modern day sculptors and the like try and capture some of its magic. Something special happens here within the castle walls and it is difficult to pin it down or put into words.

Emma Dent
and Busy.

It rained at Voiron all evening – seeing all Voiron under red umbrellas fired John to issue forth and purchase one – Busy our little fox terrier accompanied him and while he selected a faded one in the dim light, Busy took the opportunity of having a fracas with a large white cat in the back premises – the old wife of the umbrella vendor in her desire to save Puss snatched her up in her arms – but Puss being in a rage could not distinguish between friend and foe and in her great desire to take vengeance on Busy scratched her old mistress on hands and face... Busy came off triumphant and Master with a faded umbrella. The faded strips by the daylight of the next day were so palpable that it was necessary to return to the old man and request an exchange for a new one – so with strict instructions that Master was to hold Busy under his arm while negotiations were carried on they once more issued forth on the umbrella mission. This time a proper one was selected – the old man (to his shame let it be recorded) was delighted to see Busy, patted her most affectionately and laughing till he cried explained by signs how the cat had scratched the old woman and how grateful he was to Busy for being the instrument of so doing – suggestive of the old woman having scratched him occasionally and now the compliment had been returned, without his having had the trouble to do it.

Zabik
August 2009

Opening one's house to the public involves many enjoyable encounters with visitors, but occasionally an awkward situation can arise.

Pets and animals have always been a feature of our life here at Sudeley and in this case I am referring to an embarrassing moment that happened thirteen years ago but seems almost like yesterday, which involved my adored, but sometimes unmanageable, Samoyed, Zabik.

Zabik was either loved or feared by all who crossed his territory. If you were human and kept your feet from entering his den under the kitchen table when he was in residence, or you didn't reprimand him for stealing your sandwich or leg of lamb from the sideboard or ask that he vacate your favourite chair by the fire or present a territorial challenge of any sort, and particularly if you were not an alpha male of the canine species, you stood a chance of not trying his patience and could be honoured as one of his mates.

Samoyeds are an ancient breed of dog, a cross between a Spitz and a Siberian Wolfhound bred to work with and provide security for their Siberian masters. They developed a strong upper body to pull heavy timber sledges across the tundra, retained their wolfish teeth to tear apart raw meat and their thick and luxuriant coats provided wool for clothing and to insulate the yurts against sub-zero temperatures. They also liked sleeping in the comfort of their human's bed, humans they considered not as masters but providers. Zabik retained most of these inherited qualities, which his human friends were advised to respect. Amongst his many interests he was also a connoisseur of fine leather and fabric. Friend or foe alike could not escape his fascination with their cashmere shawls, best shoes, or other articles of clothing.

In 1996 I was asked to contribute a short piece to an amusing collection of behind-the-scenes stories from stately home owners entitled *Stately Secrets* by Richard, Earl of Bradford. My contribution followed a recent unfortunate incident with a Scottish visitor, which I hoped would be a one-off bit of mischief from my exuberant Samoyed puppy.

At six months our Samoyed Zabik had developed into a large and lovable bundle of white fur, with a penchant for chewing fine fabrics. One warm autumn afternoon, we were outside enjoying a game of tug-of-war, when at the far end of the garden appeared a distinguished looking Scotsman dressed in an elegant kilt. Studiously absorbed in his guidebook, he did not notice Zabik break away from our frolic and bound across the lawn towards him – until it was too late. The Samoyed too quickly had sunk his teeth into the tartan delicacy, and was yanking at it in the manner in which we had been playing.

When I arrived on the scene I realized that the Scotsman was not in a sporting mood. Wrestling with an over-assertive sledge-dog was perhaps not his idea of a good day out, and, to be sure, there was no mention of it in the guidebook.

After a prolonged and embarrassing struggle on my knees, I finally extracted Zabik's sharp teeth from the material and began a hasty retreat, offering sincere apologies for my pet's behaviour, but noticing as I did so that a sizable chunk of the gentleman's kilt was missing.

Missing but not lost – there seemed to be something colourful hanging out of the side of my dog's mouth. I thought it best not to draw attention to our visitor's now flawed attire; I was still counting on the fact that he hadn't recognised me as the mistress of the house.

My hopes for that remaining an isolated incident were sadly unfulfilled. Zabik's reputation as an incorrigible scoundrel grew in the neighbourhood and until this day he is still remembered as a local character. His daughter Kola who lives with me now has a much gentler nature and not the same wicked sense of humour, perhaps because she takes after her mother, a kind and hard working sheep dog, who in a rash moment forgot her virtue and fell for the charms of the handsome white suitor who came to call in the night.

Elizabeth with Susan Hampshire during the filming of *The Pallisers*.

It's A Wrap

For over 1,000 years Sudeley has played numerous and varied roles in local and national history and in this column I have referred to many of the illustrious personalities and momentous events that have made the castle such a unique and fascinating historic landmark.

It has as well been an inspiration for the creative imagination of writers and more recently film makers as a suitable location for their stories. P.G. Wodehouse saw Sudeley as Blandings Castle where Lord Emsworth housed and idolised his prize pig, the Empress of Blandings, while a feature length film of *Beauty and the Beast* starring George C. Scott transformed the Banqueting Hall into the Beast's enchanted castle.

I admit to being somewhat star struck, a weakness left over from my adolescence when I sneaked off to watch Elizabeth Taylor and Montgomery Cliff in awe on location near my Southern home, filming the romantic Civil War Epic *Raintree County*. Over the years at Sudeley I have delighted in meeting the actors in the filming of such popular TV productions of the classic's, including Dickens's *Martin Chuzzlewitt*, Jane Austen's *Pride and Prejudice* and *Emma*, P.G. Wodehouse's *Heavy Weather* with Peter O'Toole who reported it as 'The Dream Role', wandering around the castle as the balmy Lord Emsworth. Scenes from David Starkey's *Six Wives of Henry VIII* used Sudeley as a backdrop for several productions and for a time exquisitely dressed Tudor ladies floated timelessly around the gardens as if in a flashback to the castle's sixteenth-century heyday.

Perhaps the filming that I most enjoyed witnessing, and which showed Sudeley at its best, was *The Pallisers*, based on the political novels of Anthony Trollope. Produced and broadcast in the mid-1970s, it was a delight to recently watch the series again on DVD. Sudeley played the part of Omnium Castle, the seat of Plantagenet Palliser and his spirited wife Lady Glencora, where elegantly dressed ladies and gentlemen took tea in the gardens and serious political debates were held in the library. With the talented cosmetic skills of the set designers, part of the castle was miraculously transformed into the Houses of Parliament with shouting and riots taking over as the country headed towards political crisis.

A real life drama developed during one evening's filming in the ruins, when Lady Glencora, played by Susan Hampshire, let out an unscripted shriek and fled the scene. She reported seeing one of our resident bats flying about above her and that it swooped into the proximity of her hair. Bat lovers claim the accusations of hair entangling is an old wives' tale and bats are the good guys, very helpful to us in so many ways, but I too feel wary of those mouse like furry little creatures flying blindly around in the still of the night, so am in sympathy with 'Lady Glencora' in her distress.

Sudeley, like other large country houses hungry for income, welcomes the interest of film companies, but a production can sometimes turn into a two edged sword. The owner is bounced from his own territory and a large and loud production team takes over with cables and sharp edged equipment, moving priceless treasures around to their liking, seeming to ignore nervous appeals like 'please be careful with that Sèvres vase'!

However, all the above and more make for rarely a dull moment at Sudeley, and the star struck owner might dream on for a lucrative romantic block buster starring Piers Brosnan or Brad Pitt to come her way.

* * *

IT'S A WRAP in cinematic terms means the work is done, and this wraps up a collection of short essays on my life and observations of the day-to-day comings and goings at Sudeley Castle with a glimpse into its long and fascinating history. It has been fun to write it all down and an invigorating preamble to the next project, a full and in depth exploration of twentieth-century Sudeley.

Richard Briers and Peter O'Toole star in *Heavy Weather*.

About the Author

Elizabeth Ashcombe has been the guiding light at Sudeley Castle for the past forty years.

Arriving in England as the young American bride of Mark Dent-Brocklehurst she and their children, Henry and Mollie, inherited the Castle on his untimely death in 1972. Over the years Sudeley Castle has become one of England's most popular historic houses and has won several garden awards.

In 1979 Elizabeth married Lord Ashcombe and in the early 1980s they together carried out major refurbishment to the Castle in an attempt to strike a balance between a visitor attraction and what remains primarily a family home.